MIND MATTERS

By

Richard Olley

This book is dedicated to my grandfather, Lionel Everest Bennett, whose unconditional love meant more to me than he ever knew.

List of Contents

FOREWORD 1

Introduction 3

Chapter 1 - The subconscious mind 8

Chapter 2 - Repressions, core beliefs and neuroses 29

Chapter 3 - Making sense of relationships 68

Chapter 4 - The hidden programs that determine our behaviour
.... 99

Chapter 5 - Self-love and self-forgiveness 120

Chapter 6 - Your mind and your health 136

Chapter 7 - Time for some solutions 162

Chapter 8 - Hypno-analysis - the cream of therapies 180

Chapter 9 - The art of self-hypnosis 197

Chapter 10 - The surprising sources of our deeper instincts,
drives and feelings 210

Conclusion 226

Appendix - Resolving problems with alcohol 236

Bibliography 260

FOREWORD

This book takes you on a real journey of discovery, taking in all the 'sights' of the subconscious mind and introducing therapeutic tools you may well have never considered – or even heard of.

Richard Olley has experienced many of life's problems from the inside, so he has the insight and understanding that can only come from personal experience and shows clearly how properly applied therapy can literally turn somebody's life around. He weaves his own story with a clear explanation of the sheer power of subconscious self-limiting beliefs and how they can seriously affect every aspect of our lives - and why it's often so very difficult to make changes on our own.

Then comes the important question: who is actually in charge of your life - you, or your subconscious mind? You'll discover that the subconscious has an awful lot to answer for. Better yet, you'll soon begin to understand how your own mind and thought processes have thus far been governed by the unhelpful 'stuff' that your subconscious has learned. Explanations of repressions, core beliefs, neuroses, libidic energy and even Sigmund Freud's ideas are all here, seasoned with Richard's personal story and fascinating case studies from his experience as a therapist.

Among the interventions explored is hypno-analysis – the 'cream of therapies' as it's referred to here. And with good reason; if there's a belief that is without foundation, an anxiety without cause, a stultifying phobia, or panic attacks that just flare up with no warning, hypno-analysis can produce some incredible results. So much so that sometimes the individual concerned will be convinced that he was 'never all that bad in the first place...'

This is a great read that explains complex ideas in an accessible way, from the different ways that the subconscious mind can sabotage our lives to how we can get the most out of some of the available therapies. And if you're not keen on presenting yourself to a real live therapist yet, there's even a self-help chapter that will teach you how to use self-hypnosis.

Richard Olley has produced a concise work that expertly covers far more ground than you might at first realise, with introductions to many therapeutic techniques – prepare to be enlightened!

Terence Watts

Chairman of The Association for Professional Hypnosis and Psychotherapy
Chairman of The National Register of Psychotherapists and Counsellors
Fellow of The National Register of Advanced Hypnotherapists
Fellow of The Royal Society of Medicine
Freeman of the City of London

Introduction

I spent most of my working life as a tree surgeon, abseiling around trees with a chainsaw. I had always enjoyed climbing trees as a child, and it seemed to me to be the perfect job. Generally speaking I enjoyed my working life, and with the exception of a few accidents and injuries, my career went reasonably according to plan. I cannot make the same claim for my personal life – it was, frankly, a complete and utter shambles.

Having been divorced in my early thirties, I spent the next twenty years living an adrenaline-fuelled life strewn with danger, disastrous decisions and broken relationships. I was snappy, unreasonable, needy and unsettled. The fact that my life was not following the path I had hoped for did not escape my attention, but I figured that I was just unlucky, accident prone and a bad judge of character. Without fail, all my relationships ended in tears, sometimes mine but usually theirs. I put this down to the fact that all women were just fundamentally mad.

Eventually the truth dawned on me – I was creating all this chaos myself. I was running on a series of subconscious programs that were attracting me to danger as well as making me choose partners who had specific types of emotional damage. I now understand that it is not that some people are lucky in life and others aren't, it is that some people are programmed to make good decisions, and others are programmed to self-sabotage. There were events hidden deep in my past that had installed subconscious programs which kept attracting me to danger and disaster, in my pastimes and my relationships.

In this book I look back over a somewhat colourful life and explain how what I learned about human behaviour eventually gave me a deep personal insight into the chaos of my own life. The knowledge I gained eventually allowed me to completely turn my life around and change career from arborist to hypno-analyst. I now help other people to benefit from the insights I gained, and assist them to turn their own lives around in the same way that I have done. I am now happier, calmer and more fulfilled than I have ever been, and I am also much less likely to have a serious accident!

Our lives effectively run on programs which are often installed in our subconscious minds inadvertently. If you are unlucky enough to have some self-sabotaging programs installed, you will keep making the same mistakes - as the saying goes 'if you do what you've always done, you'll get what you've always got'. The good news is that it is perfectly possible to find out what these programs are, and to exchange the unhelpful ones for more positive programs that will literally change the path of your life.

Inevitably, as I describe the problems that dogged me from my childhood, I will appear to be criticising my parents and their child-rearing abilities. This is not my intention at all. I grew up in what was to me a rural paradise, I was educated well and I was taught the value of money and the importance of hard work, honesty and integrity. I am genuinely grateful to my parents for these things. Above all, my parents, who thankfully are still alive at the time of writing, parented me according to the received wisdom of the day.

However, there were times when I was 'encouraged' not to express my emotions, and it is only looking back that I can see that I was loved – there were particular circumstances that prevented me from seeing this at the time. For reasons that I will explain in detail in the book, it doesn't much matter what happens to you in your life – but what is crucially important is what you *think* about what happens to you. This is because your thoughts create your emotions, and it is your emotional damage that adversely affects your future. But my point here is that no one involved was in any way aware of the subconscious programs that were being installed in my young mind, and being unaware, they were, by definition, not responsible.

While we obviously cannot be consciously aware of what our subconscious programs are, there are fairly simple ways of finding out. This book is about how I identified the programs I was running on, and how I changed them. It describes my own path of self-discovery, and in doing so, it gives the reader the directions to embark on a similar journey themselves.

The subconscious programs I refer to caused me to frequently indulge in high risk behaviour, make bad decisions, lack self-love, drink too much and lurch from one dysfunctional relationship to another. After many years I could not escape the obvious fact that the only thing that all my disasters, near-misses and broken relationships had in common was me. I was the only common denominator. In my early fifties I recognised that change was well overdue, but I didn't know where to start or how to do it.

During this long process of self-discovery, I read widely on subjects as diverse as anthropology, addiction, microbiology, neurology, psychology, hypnotism and many others. I also went on many courses, learning about Psychological Kinesiology, Emotional Freedom Therapy, the Lightning Process, psychotherapy, hypnotherapy and hypno-analysis. I find human behaviour fascinating, and I embarked on this journey because there were many things about my own behaviour - and that of my partners - that I struggled to make any sense of at all. However, once I eventually figured out what drove my chaotic behaviour, I turned everything around in a year. I am now calm, non-judgemental, happy in my own skin and I choose not to drink alcohol.

The knowledge I gained through reading and attending courses helped me to identify my underlying problems, and resolve them once and for all. I have included many key revelations in this book, both because I found them very interesting, and because I think they will directly help others to make similarly positive changes in their lives. Despite the fact that I am now a therapist, I have written this book in layman's language because I want anyone to be able to understand the messages and the processes, and to follow the path I took.

Many people suspect that they need to make some fundamental changes to get their lives on track, but they have absolutely no idea how to do it. They read self-help books, but can't relate what they read to the nuts and bolts of their own lives. They might even have some counselling, and gain some insight as to why they are the way they are, but that knowledge does not necessarily facilitate fundamental change.

In this book I describe how and why your subconscious mind so often sabotages what you consciously want, and I give practical advice on what to do about it. I have to own up to occasionally swerving off the main theme of the book where interesting side topics catch my attention – hopefully you will share my enthusiasm and consider the diversions justified.

Chapter 1

The subconscious mind

The scale and influence of the subconscious mind

Many great books have been written about the power of the subconscious mind. Most of these books are about how to harness that power by making it work in our favour - in other words, they encourage us to accept and repeat life-enhancing core beliefs in the hope that our lives will be transformed by this new positivity coming from deep inside us. Our core beliefs are subconsciously held and are our fundamental views about ourselves and the world around us. In my opinion, simply trying to 'instal' positive beliefs is the wrong approach, and it is frequently doomed to fail.

Let me explain why. For most people, far and away the greatest influence that their subconscious core beliefs and programs have on their lives is a negative one. These limiting and negative attitudes have usually been inadvertently installed, mostly in childhood. I refer to them as 'programs' because our subconscious mind is very much like a self-programming computer, and this ability of the human mind to re-program itself according to how life unfolds around us is at once a great strength and a terrible weakness. For instance, if we encounter a danger in our environment, we can develop an instinctive fear of it, which is helpful to our survival. But the same process can malfunction and give us irrational fears and phobias which can be very limiting. The programs are mostly very simple, and by definition, since they are subconscious, we cannot be consciously aware of them. It is also important to understand that the subconscious mind is immensely more powerful than the conscious mind, and will always win when the two have conflicting agendas.

Limiting or negative core beliefs could include 'I am unlovable', 'I am stupid', or 'I will never be a success', for example. Negative programs are reactive, which is to say that a given stimulus will always produce a given response, and they are often linked to negative core beliefs. If your experience is that intimate relationships usually end painfully, your 'programming' could be to sabotage any such relationship as soon as intimacy develops in order to avoid getting hurt again. They can also become self-fulfilling prophecies – if you believe that men are fundamentally untrustworthy, you may be attracted to untrustworthy men and your belief becomes successively reinforced as your life unfolds.

The key point is this: if you try to instal positive programs which are the opposite of the pre-existing negative ones, it is hardly surprising that they don't work. The existing negative ones will have potentially been in place for decades, and as I have just explained, are also likely to have been regularly reinforced over that period. A much more intelligent approach is to find out what the existing negative programs are, and 'uninstal' them.

I am reminded of the old adage – 'don't try harder, try smarter'. Most of us know from personal experience that trying harder to change deeply-wired behaviour rarely works. Think about trying to diet, to drink less alcohol, to stop nail-biting, to make better relationship choices, to have more personal confidence. These areas of our lives are all controlled by our subconscious mind, and we will very rarely win a fight with our own subconscious in the long run. So this book offers the 'try smarter' approach. Often, all that is necessary to effect enormous positive change is to un-instal negative programs, for the simple reason that our 'natural' state, our 'default setting' if you like, does not include these behaviours.

I promised in the preface to keep this book free from psychological jargon, and I will, but I do need to start by explaining the concept of the subconscious mind and its relationship with our conscious thoughts. Most of us know what we mean by our 'consciousness' – simply put, it is what we are *aware* of thinking about on an ongoing basis. While we are awake, our conscious mind is usually busy analysing what people have said, making everyday decisions and planning for future events.

If we work hard and lead complex lives, our conscious mind will be kept very busy.

However, our subconscious mind is far more powerful and far busier. A conservative estimate puts it as being at least a hundred times more powerful than our conscious mind, although it is obviously impossible to measure this objectively. This estimate is based upon the sheer volume of simultaneous functions which it constantly performs on our behalf, but the true figure is probably vastly greater than this. Think of your conscious mind as being like the small tip of a very, very large iceberg. The bit you can see is undoubtedly very important, but it is almost insignificant in scale and influence compared to the part you can't see.

We often hear people say that they are in two minds about something. This is probably more literally true than they think – their conscious mind is telling them one thing, and their subconscious is telling them another. No wonder they don't know what to do!

The functions of the subconscious mind

These include:

1. Controlling our autonomic processes, such as breathing, heart rate, body temperature, etc. These bodily systems are monitored and adjusted constantly, but *unconsciously*.

2. Monitoring our environment – it is alert to all available sensory information, and only makes us consciously aware of what it thinks is most important.

3. It appears to have a major role in memory formation and storage, although this is not well understood.

4. Reading other people's body language for us, and providing 'instinctive' feelings about them, if we care to listen.

5. Influencing our choice of mate, as described later.

6. Apportioning our libidic energy, which is not just limited to our sex drive. Libidic energy is the psychic energy which drives all of our survival instincts as well as our sexual activity.

7. Urging us to comply with our instinctive programs, such as procreation.

8. Installing and controlling habits, which can either be a good or a bad thing.

9. Converting our thoughts to feelings, which are designed to facilitate appropriate actions, and also creating feelings from sensory information.

10. And probably most important of all, trying to keep us safe at all times, although its perception of risk is sometimes wildly different from our conscious perception. Phobias are a good example of this.

All of the items listed above have one thing in common – in some way or another, they contribute to our survival. Attempting to ensure our survival is the most basic function of the subconscious mind, but for reasons that will become apparent, it can become deeply 'misguided' about how to achieve this. For example, the subconscious mind of an agoraphobia sufferer has become convinced that open spaces present a potentially deadly threat, and no amount of logic or effort will change that belief. A 'faulty' program has been installed. So your subconscious mind acts like a well-meaning friend – always trying to help, but sometimes inadvertently doing exactly the opposite.

There are three different types of faulty programs that can become installed, and I examine each of them in detail in the following chapters. Between them, they have the potential to completely sabotage our conscious desires, and sadly they can condemn us to a lifetime of under-achievement, unhappiness and failed relationships. They can cause us to:

1. Hold negative core beliefs.
2. Have the tendency to be attracted to familiar characters and situations, despite our conscious desire for change.
3. Follow certain patterns of behaviour that we consciously wish to avoid.

A few key features of the subconscious to bear in (conscious) mind

The subconscious mind doesn't think - it is not designed to. It really is like a computer running literally hundreds of simultaneous programs which are designed to keep us safe and help us to cope with the dangers and difficulties of life.

Although it stores memories, it has no past or future – it operates only in the present tense. It is also very literal – when we communicate with it we have to word the ideas we are introducing very carefully. These new ideas are referred to as hypnotic suggestions. The subconscious also continues to work while we sleep. You might stay asleep through the sound of a storm, but most people would wake up if their bedroom doorknob was slowly turned in the night.

The subconscious also has no understanding of negatives. Again, this is an important point to understand. If you want to remember something, then repeat 'I will remember to…' not 'I must not forget to…' because your subconscious ignores the word 'not' and you are simply programming yourself to forget. Better still, bearing in mind the previous paragraph, use the present tense. Simply say 'I remember to…'

Probably most important of all, the subconscious cannot tell reality from unreality – this is a point which we will come back to later in the book. If you visualise something, your subconscious mind thinks it is actually happening, and this can work for or against you. If you don't believe this, why does your adrenaline rise when you see something frightening on TV? Consciously, you know it is only a film, but your subconscious reacts to it and releases adrenaline because it treats the visualisation as reality.

What is the relationship between the conscious mind and the subconscious?

Between the conscious mind and the subconscious mind lies a filter, which is referred to as the Conscious Critical Faculty (CCF). Like the subconscious, the CCF is of course a concept, not a structure, but it helps us to understand and explain how our core beliefs often remain unchanged throughout our lives.

It develops gradually from the age of about three onwards, and is fully in place by about the age of about seventeen. Before the age of three, children will believe pretty much anything you tell them. Throughout their childhood they become gradually less gullible as their CCF develops, until as adults, they are hopefully able to make accurate judgements about what to believe, and what not to believe. What they are actually doing at this point is comparing new information, which is above the filter, to their pre-existing beliefs, which are below the filter. At this point the CCF performs two functions:

1. Once adulthood has been achieved, the CCF prevents new information from becoming 'core beliefs'. Except in exceptional circumstances, your core beliefs are fairly fixed by the late teens, and the CCF is therefore, in a sense, the guardian of your subconscious beliefs. In theory this is a good thing, and it saves a lot of time. When new information is presented to us, we do not need to evaluate it from first principles – we simply compare it to what we already 'know', and then accept or reject it. However, if our core beliefs are faulty, we can spend our lives making decisions that are not truly in our best interests.

2. The CCF also prevents us from having access to all of our memories, and more importantly perhaps, the exact

emotions attached to those memories. It is not hard to see that sometimes, while we need to learn lessons from unpleasant experiences, we would be better off not having brilliant recall of particularly traumatic situations, and especially of their attendant emotions.

One of the clever things about the subconscious mind is that if it wants you to do something, it puts the idea into your conscious mind so that you think it is what you consciously want. Some people constantly switch backwards and forwards from consciously-driven to subconsciously-driven behaviour, and when the conscious and subconscious have widely different agendas, this can be very confusing for people around them. To the person doing this, the change is completely seamless and they are totally unaware of it. For this reason, it is easier to spot when this happens with someone else than it is when you do it yourself. Imagine that you have a partner who is generally loving, but just when the relationship is going really well, they sabotage it. The likelihood is that they consciously want the relationship, but their subconscious is not at all happy about it. Maybe the last time they fell in love they got very badly hurt, so their subconscious is trying to prevent their becoming vulnerable to a similar situation.

In the following chapters, I explain how these stimulus-response programs become installed, and later in the book, I look at how to uninstal them. This process is the key to becoming emotionally mature and happy in your own skin, and it equips you to enjoy consistently loving and intimate relationships.

What is a habit?

Habits are another example of subconscious stimulus-response programs, and to understand the nature of habits, we need to understand the 'Hierarchy of Knowledge'. There are four stages – let us examine them in the context of changing gear in a manual car:

1. Unconscious ignorance – this is a state where we are so ignorant of something that we don't even recognise that we don't know it. A small child being driven by her mother in a car would be in this state.

2. Conscious ignorance – this is where we know that something exists, but we are aware of our complete ignorance about it. An older child might observe the gear change process, but have no idea what it was about.

3. Conscious knowledge – at this point we have learned about the subject, but have to think to do it. So now we are learning to drive, and each time the engine revs are high or low, we think 'lift the accelerator, depress the clutch, shift the gear up or down, lift the clutch, re-apply pressure to the accelerator'.

4. Unconscious knowledge – at this point we can perform the task unthinkingly. So we change gear while simultaneously negotiating a junction and chatting to our friend in the passenger seat.

Level 4 tasks are ones that have been taken over by the subconscious mind, and this has the obvious advantage of freeing up the conscious mind for less routine tasks that cannot be 'automated'. The tasks are triggered by specific circumstances – in this case the engine revs being too high or too low. This is a good example of a simple subconscious program – if 'x' happens, do 'y'. So when the trigger, 'x', occurs, we feel a compulsion to perform the activity, 'y'. If we try to resist the habit, the subconscious applies pressure in the form of a craving, until we comply. By definition, if habits seemed easy to break, they wouldn't serve their purpose.

One of the functions of the subconscious mind is to recognise routine tasks in our daily lives and automate them wherever possible. It is a great system, unless of course you inadvertently automate a process that you do not wish to continue! If you routinely open and consume a bottle of wine with your evening meal, your mind will soon spot the pattern and it will not be long before you find yourself doing it whether you think it is a good idea or not. The meal becomes the trigger, 'x', and drinking the wine becomes the activity, 'y'.

We all exhibit habitual behaviour of one sort or another on a daily basis, and it can be very deeply ingrained. I once heard Jeremy Clarkson report that one of his colleagues had accepted a challenge from another crew member to see if he could drive to work with his legs crossed i.e. using his right foot on the clutch, and his left on the brake and accelerator. There are no prizes for guessing the outcome of this stupidity - he crashed. *Quelle surprise!* Any person with the slightest idea of how deeply wired our habits become could have predicted what would happen as soon as the challenge was uttered.

So who is actually in charge most of the time?

If you think it's your conscious mind, think again. For a start, you are only aware of anything in your environment if your subconscious mind chooses to make you aware of it. If the police ask a group of witnesses to describe an accident they just saw, they will all describe it differently – not because any of them are wrong, but because their individual subconscious minds chose to alert them to different aspects of the event. Under hypnosis, which effectively enables interrogation of the subconscious record, there will be much more coherence between their stories. People can, for instance, recall number plates under hypnosis that they took no conscious notice of. This is because the subconscious noticed the number plate, but saw no reason to alert the conscious mind to it. The reason that this extra information becomes available under hypnosis is that when people are hypnotised, which is effectively just a state of deep relaxation, the CCF is bypassed, and the contents of the subconscious can be accessed.

It is also true that a lot of the decisions that we *think* we make consciously are actually driven by subconscious programs that we are totally unaware of. For example, when we are single, most of us know the experience of hugging a potential partner, and noticing that they smell amazing, so we ask them out. We naturally assume that we are consciously *choosing* them. What is actually happening is that we have just breathed in their pheromones, which contain their DNA and also chemical indicators of what diseases they are resistant to. Our subconscious mind almost instantly compares their DNA and their immunities with our own, and works out whether they would be a good mate for breeding purposes. In other words, how likely our offspring are to be healthy. The more variation there is in our respective DNA, the more 'hybrid vigour' our children will display, and the higher will be their chances of survival. This is obviously the opposite of inbreeding which causes birth defects and low survival rates. It may be that this is also why we often don't particularly like the smell of our close relatives – they would be genetically the worst possible people to breed with. So next time you choose a partner, don't fool yourself about who or what actually made the decision.

Case study – Sally

Anorexia is a good example of a behaviour which is driven by the subconscious mind. It is clearly not in the sufferer's interests to starve themselves, but their subconscious mind has decided to 'over-control' their intake of food.

A twenty-eight-year-old lady called Sally came to see me recently and she had been anorexic for five years. She was extremely slim and was on the verge of being hospitalised. Several counsellors had been unable to help her. As I expected, when I asked her what had been going on in her life when the problem started, she recounted an unrelated chain of events which were unfortunate and upsetting: a bereavement, a relationship breakup, a health issue, a family problem. Individually, she would probably have coped with them and moved on. But coming all together was too much – she really felt that her life was out of control.

This situation is a typical trigger for anorexia, and her subconscious mind decided to take strict control of her eating – one assumes this is so that a person can prove to themselves that they are not completely out of control. The outcome of this will be familiar to many people. As she lost weight, the people who cared about her urged her to eat. But in order to prove to herself that she was in control, and they were not, she had to do the opposite. If she had listened to them, the control would have been theirs, and she had to avoid this at all costs. So she ate less and less, and the problem worsened. Such input from friends and families is well-intentioned, and totally understandable, but it is completely counterproductive.

I started by asking her to recount each event during the period in question, under hypnosis, and we 'reframed' each one in turn. We then put various strategies in place to help her recovery, such as asking everyone around her to 'get off her back' and completely ignore the issue, putting away her scales and covering up all the full-length mirrors in the house. While she was under hypnosis, I used a logical arguing technique (called a polybind) to help her to see the complete illogicality of her current situation. She gradually came to see that her current strategy did not represent her being in control – in fact *it* was controlling *her*, and preventing her from having the energy to enjoy her life. We then concentrated on what the benefits of eating healthily would be – what her life would be like if she truly had control. For instance, she could start wearing and looking good in her favourite dress, she could start teaching gymnastics again. At the start of her sixth session she came in and said 'I don't know what you've done to me, but I really am eating normally again'. This is an excerpt from her subsequent letter to me:

"After six sessions, my controlling and destructive anorexic mind was finally silenced. I no longer count the calories when I want to eat. I no longer lie awake at night thinking I look like an elephant. This is the most amazing feeling and I am back to thinking and behaving like the old me. A weight has truly been lifted off my shoulders and mind."

Case studies like this demonstrate two key points. The first is that the subconscious mind is enormously powerful and can become 'programmed' in ways that lead us into behaviour that is illogical and destructive and can cause us great unhappiness. The second is much more positive – using hypno-analysis we can find these programs and delete them! It shows that we really can resolve such deeply rooted behaviour that is compromising our health and happiness, and get on with enjoying our lives.

Can we bypass the Conscious Critical Faculty as adults?

If we are so clearly at the mercy of these hidden programs, is there any way to bypass the Conscious Critical Faculty and change the programs? Thankfully, yes – there are two situations where this is clearly possible. One happens naturally, and the other is created therapeutically.

1. The 'natural' way of bypassing the CCF occurs at times of high emotion – it occurs typically, but not exclusively, *when we are very afraid.* The advantages of this are obvious – you can become instantly 'programmed' to fear, and

therefore to avoid, this situation in the future. For example, if you are involved in a serious, life-threatening car accident, your subconscious mind might decide that driving should be avoided in future. You might have enjoyed driving up that point in your adult life, but the fact that your survival came into question could easily prompt your subconscious mind to change its ideas about this. It could easily generate a fear or a phobia of driving, to dissuade you from endangering yourself in future. This would be a new subconscious program, or core belief, which is planted below the CCF at a time of high emotion.

2. The therapeutic means of bypassing the CCF is under hypnosis. In the hypnotic state, the CCF is drawn aside and information can flow freely in both directions. When we instal new core beliefs, we call the process 'hypnotherapy'. If we choose to delve deeper into the subconscious and release traumatic memories from the past and their attendant emotions, we call this hypno-analysis.

The influence of Sigmund Freud

We are all so familiar with the concept of the subconscious mind that it is easy to forget that it is just that – it is a *concept*. We cannot actually prove that it exists at all – no one has ever seen one – but as a method of analysing and explaining human behaviour, it is an invaluable concept to work with. Its existence was first suggested by Sigmund Freud, one of the fathers of modern psychology. His book *The Psychopathology of Everyday Life* is still considered a classic.[1]

Freud really was a genius, and is widely credited with transforming our understanding of human behaviour, even if some of his wackier theories have now largely been discredited. His problem was that he had a tendency to formulate untestable theories on the basis of his observations, and then rely on them. For example, he was right to notice that there were several distinct character types among humans, but almost certainly wrong to attribute them to traumas that may have occurred at key moments in childhood when we were being toilet trained, or discovering that it felt nice to touch our genitals. These character types are discussed in more detail at the end of Chapter 3.

Many of Freud's observations were extremely shrewd, and he often figured out how the mind worked by studying how it malfunctioned – a very illuminating method also used much more recently to study brain function and neuroplasticity by such eminent neuroscientists as Paul Bach-y-Rita and V S Ramachandran. If you have any interest in this subject, Norman Doidge's book *The Brain that Changes Itself* is extremely interesting.[2]

Further reading

If the subject of the extraordinary power and hidden influence of the subconscious mind interests you, I would recommend *Incognito* by David Eagleman.[3] Like many good writers, Eagleman explains a complex subject well, with plenty of interesting stories and analogies that are easy to relate to. To give a completely random example of subconsciously-driven behaviour, Eagleman explains that people are statistically more likely to marry partners whose name begins with the same letter as theirs, like Janet and John, than would occur by chance. They are also more likely to choose jobs which sound like their name, like Dennis the dentist, and Laura the lawyer. The supposition is that there is a certain familiarity about this, and as will be explained many times in the following chapters, for reasons of survival, the subconscious mind is deeply wired to attract us to familiar situations.

Another bizarre example of how susceptible our behaviour is to subconscious cues is described in the results of a study by scientists in New Mexico. It turns out that the tips received by strippers varied from \$35 per hour to \$68 per hour depending on the time in their menstrual cycle that they were performing. Strippers on birth control showed no such variation and averaged \$37 per hour. The tipping customers could not have consciously known what influenced their generosity - or lack of it.

Eagleman also explains that many tasks are much better left to the subconscious, and gives a charming example of a centipede who is walking along quite happily until a passing frog asks him how he knows which foot to move when. As soon as the centipede's conscious mind attempts this task, he ends up in a ditch! Don't actually try this, but the same thing would happen to you if you decided to choose which foot to use on which stair as you ran up or down the stairs.

Chapter 2

Repressions, core beliefs and neuroses

How does the subconscious mind become programmed?

To understand how the subconscious mind can inadvertently work against our best interests, we need to start with an understanding of how it is supposed to work. As babies, we are born with some information 'pre-installed' – these are what we refer to as our instincts. They include the operation of our autonomic processes, like crying when we are hungry, or flinching away from external sources of pain. But in order to grow up and thrive in a complex world, we have to have the ability to learn very fast indeed; we have an enormous amount of information to take on board.

So it is essential that young children have the ongoing ability to absorb large amounts of new data. However, at this age, by definition, they do not have the ability to judge the accuracy of that data. Theoretically at least, this should not be a problem because they should be growing up in the care of adults who can perform this function for them. These primary caregivers, usually their parents, should have their best interests at heart, and could therefore be expected to ensure that the children learn positive, accurate and useful life lessons and skills. This, of course, assumes that the primary caregivers have these skills in the first place – unfortunately this is not always the case.

Up to the age of about three, children have virtually no ability to judge the truth of what they are told. They believe what they hear and it becomes 'the truth' as far as they are concerned at a deep - subconscious - level. These truths are the first of many core beliefs that will later shape their actions, and indeed their lives. This is crucial for caregivers to understand, because if you tell a two-year-old that he is stupid, he could end up believing this, and acting on it, for the rest of his life. It is an example of an extremely limiting core belief, and most parents would agree that it is frighteningly easy to say things like this.

Between the ages of about three and seventeen, children gradually develop the ability to challenge and evaluate the veracity of what they are told, but repeated messages from authority figures still get through. So if your teachers and/or parents still insist that you are stupid/bad/useless on a regular basis, then the corresponding negative core beliefs will still become installed.

The truth of what I am saying here is self-evident if you consider that when children are really small they are very suggestible, which is another way of saying that they are very gullible. You can convince a small child of just about anything. As children grow older they become gradually less suggestible as they acquire the skills to more accurately evaluate what they hear. Before the age of about six, their minds really are like sponges, and core beliefs can be installed with alarming ease. This is demonstrable by analysing brainwave states, which, in children, have a typically lower frequency than adults, but which are very much like the brainwaves of adults when they are in highly suggestible hypnotic states.

By the time we reach adulthood, the ability to evaluate new information is fully in place, but we have developed a 'shortcut' for doing this. It would be a very laborious process to have to think deeply about everything we hear and weigh up all the available evidence before we decide whether to accept it or not. So instead, we simply judge whether or not the new information fits with what we already know. In other words, we compare it with our core beliefs. This process generates three possible outcomes:

1. The new information fits with what we already know, and we accept it
2. The new information does not fit with what we already know, so we reject it
3. We have no previous experience to compare it with, in which case we will be forced to evaluate it from first principles, and accept or reject it on that basis.

One of the obvious implications of this is that if you grew up thinking that you were stupid, there is no PhD from Oxford or Cambridge that will ever make you really believe, deep down, that you are clever. You may tell yourself that you were just lucky, or that you might be ok on your specialist subject, but you are rubbish at everything else. If you grew up thinking that you were unlovable, no amount of assurances from your partner will ever make you feel differently about yourself - you might think that they had something wrong with them for even liking you, let alone loving you. However - before you get too pessimistic about this whole situation - there are very effective ways to solve these problems, it's just that overwriting the negative belief with a positive one is just too simplistic to be likely to work.

How do repressions happen?

Repression is the unconscious hiding or internalising of uncomfortable thoughts or feelings. If we feel an emotion - let us use anger as an example - there are two things we can do with it:

1. The healthy option is to acknowledge how we feel, to accept the reality of it, even if it is an unpleasant or uncomfortable feeling. We may express it by verbalising it, or by acting on it, but we may also choose not to. It is really important to understand that acknowledging it,

but choosing not to express it, does not amount to repression.

2. The unhealthy option is to repress it, and the verb 'to repress' is defined as 'to subdue by force or inhibit the expression of something'. In other words, we do not process the emotion in any way - instead we push it down inside ourselves, and it ends up in our subconscious. I explain the consequences of this in the next section.

You might think that the opposite of *repression* is *expression,* so instead of internalising the anger, you externalise it. In this scenario, in the interests of your own emotional wellbeing, you just let rip and shout at (or even hit!) anyone who annoys you. If you give this idea some serious thought, it simply cannot be what we need to do, for several reasons:

1. Imagine if everyone, in an attempt to maintain their own mental and emotional health, let rip with every emotion they experienced - anger, sorrow, guilt, and resentment, as well as all the positive emotions. It would be utter chaos, and the vast majority of interpersonal relationships would become unworkable with constant accusations, denials, blame, insults, etc.

2. If this behaviour really was beneficial to long-term health, the emotionally healthiest people in society would

have to behave more like this than the rest of us, and they clearly don't. If anything, the opposite is true.

3. Some personality types (for example the 'Charismatic Evidential', who are usually loud and dramatic) are known to be far more emotionally expressive than others (for example the Resolute Organisational, who are generally quiet and reserved), but I have never seen any statistical data that indicates that they are emotionally healthier. I explain more about personality types mentioned here towards the end of the next chapter.

When children fail to process emotions, it is usually because they are prevented from doing so by adults, either by overt physical or verbal threats, or by more subtle methods such as being made to feel guilty (in truth, no one can *make* you feel anything – more on this later). It seems very likely that these children will continue mishandling emotions in their later lives – the behaviour will become *habitual*. Looking back, I know I did this as a child, and I can see plenty of occasions in my adult life when I continued to do so.

A good example of an emotion I regularly avoided as an adult was the understandable feeling of sadness and loss when a relationship ended. Rather than process it, my instinct was always to just get back out there and find a new partner to fill the place and dull the pain. Knowing what I know now, I can see that this was not a healthy or sensible course of action. 'Rebound' relationships rarely work because our new partners are often not well-chosen, and when the relationship almost inevitably fails, it can reinforce our negative self-concept: one of life's many self-fulfilling prophecies.

Acceptance of your current reality, and experiencing it rather than fighting it, is actually not far removed from what Buddhists have been encouraging us to do for many centuries. Their philosophy - as far as my understanding goes - is that life's suffering is caused by the fact that humans never seem to accept their present reality *as it is*. If we are happy, we worry that our happiness will not last, and if we are in emotional or physical pain, we long for it to end. Indeed, we often try to shorten it, as I demonstrated by rushing to replace partners with whom I had split up.

Maybe we should keep in mind that everything in life is impermanent, including pleasure and pain. In order to take this message on board and 'go with the flow', we need to accept and feel our emotions *as they arise*. This makes much more sense than fighting them, and life might be much less of a struggle than we sometimes make it.

How do we pick up these repressions, and what can we do about them?

Human children are incredibly dependent on their parents for survival, and they always have been. We are clearly nothing like other animals whose young can be up and running an hour or two after birth. To have a successful childhood, we need to achieve two things – to be loved so that our parents look after us, and to express our emotions, so that they do not get 'trapped' and potentially cause us future emotional or physical ill-health. The problems arise where we feel we have to repress our emotions *in order to continue to be loved.* The evolutionary consequences of not being loved would have been disastrous – lack of nurture would mean lack of survival. So children will, if they have to, sacrifice the need to cry or express anger if they perceive that love will be withdrawn if they don't. To thrive, children need *unconditional love.* That is to say, the love they receive should not be conditional on them behaving the way we want them to. We certainly need to discipline them, and there will clearly be times when they make us angry, but the trouble starts if they feel that love has been withdrawn when we get angry with them. When children misbehave, we should be clear to them that we disapprove of the behaviour, but not of the person misbehaving. More than once people have told me that when they misbehaved, their parents would say things like, 'If you carry

36

on like that you are going to be looking for a new place to live'. And then these parents wonder why their children are insecure!

So what can we do if this has happened to us, and we feel that we are running on programs that continue to compromise our ability to express appropriate emotions? Chapter 7 of this book offers a range of self-help strategies, but Chapter 8 is specifically about hypno-analysis, and I consider this an ideal therapy for this scenario. Not only does it allow the release of trapped emotions, but it also provides the opportunity to conduct 'Inner Child' work on the related issues while still under hypnosis. Inner child work was originated by Dr Lucia Capacchione, and it theorises that (psychologically speaking) the child who we used to be is still within us, and can still be spoken to, cared for and healed.[4] The process is referred to as re-parenting. In my experience, this is a highly effective therapeutic combination.

What are the consequences of repression?

A repressed emotion, or repression, remains bottled up in us at a subconscious level and this can potentially have two serious consequences:

1. Firstly, at a fundamental level, the emotion becomes *part of us*. If we regularly repress anger, we are in danger of becoming a fundamentally angry person. The anger is inside us at a subconscious level and, without some

specialist therapy, it is likely to always be there. Unfortunately for the people around us, it tries to get out on a regular basis, and we have a tendency towards angry reactions where they are simply not justified. We all know people like this and sometimes we know enough about their past to know why they are like it, but often we are baffled by how disproportionate their reactions are to small provocations.

2. Secondly, and I look at this in detail in Chapter 6, there is a large and growing body of evidence that the process of repression can have serious long-term health consequences such as a higher risk of cancer or auto-immune diseases.

The trouble is that once the emotion is trapped at a subconscious level, conscious expression of it does not allow us to discharge it – it has become too deeply a part of us. Fortunately, hypno-analysis can often provide a very effective solution. In hypno-analysis you do not so much remember as *relive* the experience that trapped the emotion. This process is known as re-vivification, and when it occurs, the emotion is fully expressed and consequently released. Every time this happens, you get one step closer to being the person you would have been if you had had a less difficult childhood. You will remember from the last chapter that under hypnosis, the CCF is drawn aside and emotions previously trapped in the subconscious can be released. Freud theorised that it took libidic energy to hold repressions in place, and that their release would therefore be accompanied by a surge in this libidic energy.[5] Many of my clients have reported this to be the case.

What is libidic energy?

When people talk of libido, they are generally talking about their sex drive, but sex is only one of several areas of our lives where we express libidic energy. In psychological terms, libidic energy powers all of our instinctive survival drives and behaviours, which would include eating, working and caring for ourselves and others for example. Given that our sex drive is less important to our survival than these other functions, they are given first priority and it follows that if we overwork, our sex drive suffers first. The good news is that if a significant repression is released, the increased availability of libidic energy also tends to be expressed in our sex drive first, and the change can be very significant! Unfortunately, after a few weeks, the libidic energy becomes more evenly distributed again between the various processes that it powers. I had a female client in therapy once who went from being generally uninterested in her husband's advances, to actually making the advances herself. He was so delighted he offered to pay if she agreed to stay in therapy!

What types of event cause faulty core beliefs to become installed?

A core belief is a deeply held view about ourselves, others, or the world around us. Like repressions, they are usually formed when we are young, and if they are negative, they will impact our lives in a negative way. Typical examples would be 'I am unlovable' or 'people are untrustworthy', and phobias are also a form of core belief – 'spiders are dangerous' (so avoid them at all costs). From a therapist's point of view, there are essentially three distinct situations where negative core beliefs can originate:

1) Single trauma. This is where a single event occurs which the subconscious mind regards as traumatic. It could have been an event that was genuinely life-threatening, like a child being attacked by a dog. But it could just as easily have been a harmless event that was misinterpreted, like a child being knocked over by a boisterous dog that just wanted to play. Or it could be an event that was traumatic, but the 'wrong' lesson was learned such as when a child is bitten by a dog in a playground and subsequently the child develops a fear of playgrounds.

2) Cumulative trauma. This occurs when an unrelated set of events creates, and then reinforces, a specific belief. For example, a child's beloved pet might die, then a

40

favourite grandparent dies, then their first boyfriend leaves them. They could end up believing subconsciously that 'whatever or whoever I love, I will lose'.

3) Compound trauma. This happens when less traumatic events occur, but they occur repeatedly. An example of this would be when parents and/or teachers are regularly uncomplimentary about their child's intellectual capacity. This type of trauma is the least obviously traumatic, but often has the deepest negative effect. This is because it may have been repeated many hundreds of times over many years.

Because many of the core beliefs that the subconscious mind generates are not logical to the conscious mind, it is often extremely difficult to unravel them by conscious contemplation. For this reason we often simply cannot understand our own, or other people's, beliefs or behaviour when it is subconsciously driven. I once heard an excellent example of this.

A couple have two children – a boy and a girl. The boy is robust and they think it will do him good to go to boarding school. They think that the girl would probably thrive better in a more nurturing environment and send her to the local grammar school. The parents know their children's strengths and weaknesses, and have done their very best for them. Both children get good educations. The boy grows up thinking that he was sent away because he was loved less than his sister, and she grows up thinking that the parents loved her brother more because they paid for his education and not hers.

Nobody ever said that good parenting was easy!

Do more serious traumas cause more serious neuroses?

This can be the case, but it is not by any means always so. There is no question that very serious problems like repeated child abuse can totally wreck lives. I know people that have endured what some might consider 'low level' abuse and have subsequently suffered life-long anger and/or self-loathing that wrecks their relationships and causes deep and lasting distress, but I have also known those who have suffered immeasurably more serious traumas who are genuinely less traumatised. The reason for this is simply that what happens to you in life is much less important in terms of lasting trauma than *what you think about* what happens to you. As I said in the introduction, this is because it is our thoughts that determine our emotions, but it is our emotions that determine the extent of lasting trauma. The long-term impact of the trauma is therefore more likely to be proportional to the strength of emotion that it generated, rather than the scale of the trauma itself.

It may be the case that the ongoing trauma of something like feeling unloved for your entire childhood can often run much deeper than the trauma left by a much more serious one-off event in an otherwise happy childhood. I mentioned in the previous chapter that during childhood, repetition of messages from authority figures reinforces core beliefs – they just get hammered home deeper and deeper. Being told that you are stupid or useless is not particularly traumatic in itself, but if your parents and teachers repeated the message, at home and at school, week in, week out for fifteen years, you will be left absolutely convinced of the truth of it at a very deep level. And you obviously will not shift this belief by repeatedly telling yourself that you are the next Einstein while you stand in front of the mirror cleaning your teeth in the morning!

Why do our core beliefs matter so much?

One of my favourite sayings was by Henry Ford, the founder of the Ford Motor Company:

'Whether you think you can, or you think you can't, you are right'.

Thirty years after he started it, his company was manufacturing one third of all the world's cars.

The psychology underlying the truth of Ford's statement is simple – your subconscious mind attempts at all times to help to generate the outcomes in life that you expect. It does this because what is familiar to us is less threatening than what is unfamiliar. Surprises can be unpleasant and dangerous. Familiar situations, by contrast, we know how to handle.

So if our core belief is that 'we can't', our subconscious mind will do its best to ensure that we fail in our endeavours, however much we might consciously wish to succeed in them. As we discovered in the last chapter, the subconscious mind is far more powerful than the conscious mind, and it will win every time. This is just another example of how the 'well-meaning' subconscious mind can end up sabotaging our conscious desires on a daily basis. It is because we understand the enormous power of the subconscious mind that motivational gurus work so hard to help us to instal positive beliefs about our abilities. But as I have said before, I think it is unrealistic to expect to permanently overwrite long-established negative beliefs by simply repeating positive mantras.

Let's look at an example of this subconscious sabotage in action. Suppose you are having a friendly game of golf with a colleague who usually beats you. However, on this occasion you are really on fire, and by the halfway stage you are on course to thrash him, and you are really looking forward to it. Then, for no obvious reason, your game goes to pieces, you play the last nine holes even worse than usual, and you end up losing - again. Irrespective of the sport, most people have experienced a comparable situation. Consciously, we were looking forward to the win, but our subconscious mind knew that this was not a familiar outcome, and it compromised our performance to produce the expected end result.

As a matter of interest, a cunning solution if this happens to you is to compliment your friend on his swing and ask him to explain exactly how he hits the ball so well. Once he starts to consciously analyse how his swing is timed, his game will almost certainly go to pieces. Unsporting, but effective!

If you know that you have a negative core belief, and you need to overcome it for a specific situation, you can use visualisation. This is a great tool for temporarily reprogramming the subconscious mind to the outcome you want. If you visualise a specific outcome clearly, your subconscious mind is unable to distinguish this image from reality, and if the visualisation is powerful enough, it can temporarily change your subconscious belief of what is about to happen. Turning to golf again, if you watch a professional golfer, he will look where he wants the ball to go, and will visualise it going there. Then he puts his head down and hits the ball, trusting his body to achieve the outcome he visualised. He doesn't even think of looking at the target as he hits the ball - he trusts his body to achieve the visualisation. The same is true of a rugby player kicking a conversion – he will look at the posts and clearly visualise the ball sailing through the middle, but he keeps his head down as he kicks. Visualisation is described in greater detail later in Chapter 7.

Case study – Jill

Jill is in her fifties, and she came to see me because she had relationship issues and strong and recurrent feelings of guilt. She told me during her initial consultation that she had been a real tearaway as a teenager growing up in a deprived area of Newcastle, and had had a series of inappropriate relationships in her early twenties.

Under hypnosis, she revealed that she felt guilty about the worry and pain that her wild teenage behaviour had caused her parents. Looking back, she could see that her parents had really struggled to cope with her difficult, unruly, demanding and ungrateful behaviour. It made her feel that she was a bad person.

The truth of the matter soon emerged. At the age of thirteen she had been groomed by a paedophile who gave her clothes and sweets. A year later she found that she was pregnant and her abuser immediately disappeared. She was talked into having an abortion. Under hypnosis, I gently helped her to see that it was not her who was the 'bad person' in her story – her unruly behaviour was a perfectly normal reaction to the very unpleasant experiences that she had been subjected to.

She soon recognised that it was her core belief that she was a bad person that attracted her to men who would treat her badly, because at a deep level she felt that she deserved it. By the end of her fifth session she had a much healthier self-image and told me that she felt so much happier and at ease with herself. Her core belief about herself had really changed for the better.

How can we find out what our core beliefs really are?

If all of our core beliefs were positive, life would be so much easier! In some cases, we know that we have negative core beliefs, and we just live with the knowledge because we have no idea what to do about it. But in other cases, we have absolutely no idea that deep down, our beliefs are the polar opposite of what we consciously believe. So how can we find out what they really are?

One of the tools we can use is kinesiology. This is also known as 'muscle testing' and can be used to identify food and chemicals which the client is allergic to, as well as to find out what their core beliefs are. The theory is that if we are exposed to something we are allergic to, or if we say something that is contrary to a deeply held belief, our muscles become noticeably weaker. By pushing down on an outstretched arm which the client is attempting to hold horizontal, the therapist can feel the difference in strength. This might sound a bit 'alternative' but you may well be surprised if you try it on a friend. It may take a little practice, and they need to learn not to push up as you push down - but if they get the hang of it, you will get results.

Let me start by giving a practical example of this. In my late thirties I gradually became quite ill and was unable to work for three years. I was working as a tree surgeon at the time, which is physically demanding in the extreme. I was utterly exhausted; over the course of about a year, I went from being super-fit to being unable to walk upstairs without struggling for breath. I was in and out of London hospitals having every test you could think of, but the medical profession was baffled. I went to site some days to help organise jobs but was completely unable to undertake any physical work whatsoever. If I tried, my health became worse than ever.

The NHS spent three years trying to establish the cause of my illness, and to their credit they worked very hard at it. At one point, I had to go to a London hospital to have three muscle biopsies taken from my thigh. When I attended my appointment, I was told by the doctor that the procedure was quite unpleasant because it involved her pushing a gadget deep into my thigh muscle to extract a sample of the tissue. To make it worse, she could not use anaesthetic because it would compromise the sample she took. Worse still, she had to do this three times, in the same position, and she was honest enough to say that it got increasingly painful each time. I have to admit that she was an exceedingly attractive lady, and for some reason that I can't explain, but most guys will understand, I was absolutely determined not to show any sign of weakness during the procedure. Not one murmur was going to pass my lips, and there would be no physical reaction at all.

The first time she performed the biopsy, everything went according to plan – it was unpleasantly painful, but I kept it to myself. The second time was worse, but I still held it together. The third time was about ten times worse, and I instantly yelled a rather choice four letter word at the top of my voice as my leg shot up and hit her squarely under the jaw. I heard her teeth smash together and she staggered back across the room! My plan was in tatters. It turned out that she had gone too deep, and hit my thigh bone. I was full of apologies, worried that I had broken her jaw, and she too was full of apologies, saying it was all her fault.

As it turns out, the efforts of the NHS were in vain, and no diagnosis was forthcoming. In desperation, I went to see a kinesiologist. I relate this story because it demonstrates how kinesiology allows the therapist to 'read' information directly from your body that you are not consciously aware of, and that information can be physical or psychological.

How did the therapist figure out what was wrong with me?

She first asked me to hold out my right arm horizontally, and to try to keep it where it was while periodically testing my strength by trying to push the arm down. She started by asking me to make a series of statements, some of which we both knew to be true, and others false. Each time I made a statement, she would test the strength of my arm. Making a false statement is physically disempowering, and she was just 'calibrating' me, so that she could easily tell from my strength whether what I said was true or false. If I said my name was Richard, my arm remained strong. If I said it was Susan, my arm weakened. Once she could confidently 'read' my body's responses to the statements, she would ask me to make a statement such as 'my illness is caused by bacteria'. My arm weakened, so this clearly wasn't true.

After several other statements which also turned out to be false, she asked me to say 'I am being poisoned by a chemical'. My arm was rock solid – my body had told her a truth that I was consciously completely unaware of. The theory behind this is simple – if you say something that is in conflict with a deeply held belief, or is in conflict with a fact that your body 'knows' to be true, your muscles are noticeably weakened.

The kinesiologist then asked me to go home and get a sample of every chemical that I came into contact with and bring the samples to her in small glass bottles the following week. I took about fifty samples – absolutely anything I could think of – shampoo, milk, petrol, red wine, engine oil, washing up liquid, toothpaste, whisky, Bovril, diesel, etc. The samples were not labelled, they were numbered, so neither of us could have any pre-conceived ideas about what the outcome would be.

The next part of this process I find hard to explain – I just do not know how this worked, but I know that it did. I was lying down with my eyes shut, my arm held out horizontally. One after another, she put the little glass bottles on my chest, and tested my arm. At no point was I physically in contact with the chemicals being tested. With two of them, my arm weakened significantly, and with a third one, my arm nearly fell off! When we cross-referenced the samples to my list, all three were hydro-carbons – the first two were petrol and diesel and the one with by far the strongest reaction was chain oil.

For any non-chainsaw users reading this, (I suppose there might be some!) a chainsaw has an oil tank which feeds oil onto the moving chain to lubricate it. Unlike in an engine, this is what is known as a 'total loss system' – the oil sprays off into the atmosphere, and is constantly replaced by more from the tank. Chain oil is generally made from recycled engine oil, which mechanics are told is so carcinogenic that they should avoid getting it on their hands. Chainsaw users inadvertently inhale a mist of it for hours on end. After years of doing this, my body had clearly had enough.

I believe that my subconscious mind decided to solve the problem by rendering me completely unable to work. This is a classic example of the type of situation that Gabor Maté describes in his highly relevant book *When the Body Says No.*[6] If I didn't have the strength or energy to go to work, I couldn't use a chainsaw, and the poisoning would stop. Unfortunately I still needed to attend site and run my business, so I was still near chainsaws, and was still breathing the oil in, albeit in lower doses. Luckily for me, there is an alternative to mineral chain oil that is made from rapeseed. As a business, we changed over to it, and in a few months I was able to regain my fitness and get back to work. For the rest of my career, if a sub-contractor came on site using mineral chain oil I could tell within minutes. My throat started to ache and all the old symptoms came back. If we re-filled his saw with rapeseed oil, the problems went away just as quickly.

How does kinesiology actually work?

I know that the process I have just described sounds unconventional, but I am adamant that it works. Most people assume that their mind and their brain are effectively one and the same thing, but there is actually plenty of evidence that this is not the case. For example, if we want to know someone's deepest, intuitive thoughts about something, we ask them for their 'gut feeling'.

A more bizarre example of your body 'knowing' things is the phenomenon of cellular memory – this is where organ transplant recipients take on the memories, behaviours and even tastes of the organ donor. This is well-documented and strongly suggests that our mind is not exclusively located in our brain, but may well be distributed throughout the cells of our bodies. If this is so, it suddenly becomes much easier to understand how the function of muscle cells might be compromised by trying to work while the mind is exposed to some type of conflict or perceived danger. I personally find it easier to understand 'psychological' kinesiology than to figure out how the body can respond to the proximity of a chemical that it is not actually exposed to.

I have included a paragraph about the phenomenon of cellular memory at the end of this chapter. It is not specifically relevant unless you have had an organ transplant, but it is a fascinating subject which could potentially give us a much greater understanding of how the mind and memory actually work, and more particularly, how our thoughts could potentially affect the health of every cell in our body. Even if you don't believe this is possible, please just suspend your disbelief and keep an open mind.

Why am I telling you about my chain oil poisoning?

I have related the story for three reasons:

1. It clearly demonstrates the effectiveness of kinesiology. My particular interest is in how it can help us to 'read' the subconscious beliefs of clients. As a therapist, it is an invaluable tool for testing theories – the body is giving us information that the conscious mind does not have access to.

2. It shows how closely your health is related to your subconscious mind. My illness was unquestionably psychosomatic – it was definitely very real, but I am convinced that it was triggered subconsciously. It therefore seems very likely that the key to resolving psychosomatic illnesses also lies in the subconscious, which is why modern medicine, for all its amazing advances, has not excelled in this field. More on this subject in Chapter 6. Psychosomatic illnesses are just as

real as any others, but they are triggered, either partially or wholly, by the mind.

3. It demonstrates how your subconscious mind can take drastic action to ensure your safety when it considers that you are at risk. *'When the Body Says No'* is a great title for Gabor Mate's book, because so many of our illnesses have no obvious causative agent. The body has simply decided, *rightly or wrongly*, that we need a break. Just as with my chain oil poisoning, it seems very likely that problems like chronic fatigue syndrome and fibromyalgia are instances of the subconscious mind finding a way to stop us doing something for reasons which we do not consciously understand.

This experience of kinesiology fascinated me, but it was the possibility of finding out people's core beliefs that really grabbed my attention. I did a couple of courses in Psychological Kinesiology, a therapy originated by Robert Williams and marketed as Psych-K™. What I had not anticipated was that with a little practice, you could muscle-test yourself. Now that is a very handy tool indeed! Psych-K™ is not just a diagnostic tool – it offers ways of resolving the issues that it reveals.

Personally, I found the diagnostic element of it extremely effective, but the therapeutic processes less so. I suspect that it is a therapy that works differently for different people. I may well have been better off to have gone to an experienced practitioner, rather than trying to work on myself.

How do we actually use kinesiology to establish people's core beliefs?

It is evident from what we have discussed so far that our lives could, to a large extent, be steered by a set of negative self-beliefs that we are, by definition, unaware of. On the face of it, this is a pretty depressing situation to be in. The outcomes of our endeavours could be regularly frustrated by a subconscious mind that, in an attempt to help us, is actually sabotaging us at every turn. It is a sad fact that many people's lives follow this pattern. Deep down, they believe they will never succeed, and they never do; they believe they will never be happy, and they never are; they believe they will never meet Mr Right, and they never meet him.

The first step to resolving this situation must be to find out what your core beliefs really are. As an example, I once had a client who I knew had been abused as a child. I asked him if he (consciously) thought that he deserved to be treated with love and respect, and his response was 'of course I do'. I then asked him to hold his arm out while I 'calibrated' his strength with some questions which we both knew the answer to. When I asked him to repeat the statement 'I deserve to be treated with love and respect', his arm dropped like a stone and he burst into tears. His appalling treatment as a child had taught him, at a deep level, that he did not deserve to be treated with love and respect, and as an adult, he had chosen partners who fulfilled this expectation, not by physically abusing him, but in other ways.

Finding out the details of the limiting and potentially destructive programs that we are running is very enlightening. Start off by trying to become much more self-aware. Make a note of any surprising or unwanted emotions, and the situations that created them. Make a note of any repeating patterns that you notice in your life. If you have a really close friend who knows you inside out, enlist their help. Once you have amassed enough material for a kinesiologist to create a list of statements to test, take them to a kinesiologist who works at a psychological level.

How do negative core beliefs make our lives more difficult?

Negative core beliefs can be very damaging in many areas of our lives, but none more so than in relationships. Feeling unloved or unlovable is a common negative core belief, and it is incredibly damaging to our ability to enjoy the warmth and love we seek from having a relationship with someone else. It has been said many times that you cannot thrive in a loving relationship until you can learn to love yourself. I have tested the 'I love myself' statement many times over the years with a wide range of people, and the ones whose arms stay up are sadly in a small minority. For most people, their arm completely loses strength. I don't mind admitting that for most of my life, I could not pass this test.

If we lack a natural feeling of self-love, an obvious solution is to find a partner whose words and actions will make us feel loved. However, this strategy is fraught with problems. If we do not feel lovable, it will almost certainly be because when we were children, the significant adults in our lives failed to make us feel loved, even if we were. As we have already discussed, our subconscious mind attracts us to people with familiar characteristics, because what is familiar is, in theory at least, less threatening to us than what is unfamiliar. So unbeknown to us, we could actually be pre-programmed to choose partners who will either fail to really love us, or at least fail to make us feel loved. Because this is such a sensitive issue to us, we are very observant of any signs that they might not love us, and we frequently misread the smallest of signs - maybe they take a long time to return a text or a phone call, or maybe they appear to be flirting with someone else. Observing these signs can throw us into an instant state of panic because we know instinctively that withdrawal of love by others can have horrendous consequences.

Why is it so important to us to feel loved?

Humans are social animals, and love is the bond that holds our social groups together. We have never been a solitary species – historically we would have found it almost impossible to survive alone. The reason that having love withdrawn feels so horrible goes back to our earliest anthropological roots. Homo sapiens has been living on planet Earth for about 100,000 years, and for the vast majority of that time we have mostly existed as groups of nomadic hunter-gatherers. Our very survival depended on the bonds that held our group together - if we were cast out of the group, particularly as a child, it was effectively a death sentence. There was no social security, no larger community that could help, there was no one else who could possibly avert the impending disaster of a lingering (or not so lingering!) death. This is why, even today, being rejected by someone we love feels so utterly horrible. Anyone who has been unceremoniously dumped from a relationship that they thought was working can attest to this.

Feeling that love has been withdrawn presses the panic button in our subconscious mind. As has been previously discussed, our subconscious minds instal and run simple, stimulus-response programs of the type 'if x happens, then do y', where x is an event, and y is our response to it. When these programs are unhelpful, they are what psychologists refer to as neuroses, and they are mostly installed in childhood. When an event, or often a series of events, occurs in our childhood that generates a neurosis, by definition, our response to that particular event, or series of events, will always be the same, and will always be childish. This will continue to be the case right through into adulthood. This is a really important point to understand - without processing the neurosis to rid ourselves of it, we will rarely, if ever, be able to handle that type of event in an adult way. It is exposure to a similar event to the one that caused the problem which presses the button on a neurosis that, in turn, flips our behaviour into 'child mode'.

In the next chapter we take a quick look at Transactional Analysis – this allows us to analyse whether in any particular scenario we are triggered to behave as a Parent, an Adult or a Child.

What happens when our responses become childish?

The natural response of most children to being hurt by one of their peers is either to run away or to retaliate. So if we have a neurosis about being unlovable, these are our two instinctive options when our partner triggers pain and/or panic in us by 'making' us feel unloved. I am using quotes here because they are not actually *making* us feel unloved, they are *triggering* us to feel unloved – the emotion comes from within us and is solely generated by our thoughts about ourselves. When this happens, we either run away - possibly even dumping them before they can dump us - or we lash out, verbally or physically – we might try to make them feel guilty, we might withdraw love from them, or we might insult them. In truth, all that this type of behaviour achieves is to damage the relationship, and when the relationship eventually fails under the strain, it only serves to reinforce our belief that we are unlovable. It is another classic example of a self-fulfilling prophecy.

Let us imagine how different life might be if we did not suffer in this way - if we were able to uninstal these negative core beliefs and programs. For a start, we would naturally be attracted to people who really would love us - rather than feeding our insecurity, their behaviour would reinforce our own belief in our 'lovability'. We would be far less prone to misread events, and would naturally look for a more logical explanation of any behaviour by our partner which could potentially be misinterpreted. We would naturally respond to events in an emotionally mature way. Even if our new partner occasionally behaved illogically because of some neurosis of their own, we would not be drawn into an escalating drama. There would be no fight. We would see their behaviour for what it was, remaining calm, giving comfort and reassurance, restoring harmony as quickly as possible.

This situation is perfectly achievable - I know because I have done it, and I also know that it cannot be achieved by standing in front of a mirror and saying 'I love myself' a hundred times a day. The negative programs and core beliefs may well have been in place since childhood and will almost certainly have been reinforced many times in the intervening years. They cannot simply be overwritten - they have to be uninstalled first.

Can we inherit memories and attitudes from our parents?

We have looked at how repressions occur, and how negative core beliefs can become installed, but are there deeper ways that our subconscious can become programmed? We all know that children learn by observation, imitation and play, but could they actually be born pre-wired with any of their parents' memories and attitudes? If so, this would provide a form of 'customised instinct'. Recent experiments have shown conclusively that rats can do this. A group of rats were taught (by mildly electrocuting them) to get onto rubber pads installed in their cage whenever a specific smell was wafted through the cage. It was a smell that they had not previously encountered, and if they did not get on the pads in time, they would receive an uncomfortable electric shock through the floor of the cage. Once they had learned to do this reliably, these rats were then bred from, and then their offspring were bred from, so the next test subjects were the grandchildren of the original sample. When the smell was wafted through their cage, they headed straight for the rubber mats without their ever having 'learned' the behaviour from their own experience.

I am aware of a couple of examples that suggest that humans could possibly do this too. A good friend of mine has a very unusual phobia. Because she did not want her children to taunt her, she never discussed it with them, or with anyone else. The trigger for this phobia was a rare type of fungus that occasionally grows on large trees, so they never saw her react to it. But when her daughter was eighteen, the fungus was shown on television and she noticed that her daughter had exactly the same reaction that she did. They discussed it, and the phobic issue was exactly the same for both of them. Some instances of children having the same phobias as their parents could clearly be the result of observation, but this example appears to indicate that this is not always the mechanism involved.

The other example is something that happened to me. My mother made some reference to her father having had a heart attack many years before. I said that I remembered him coming home from hospital, and she asked me what I remembered. I told her that he was put in a bed in the living room because he couldn't climb the stairs. It was a high bed with green covers, and it was behind the door so that he had a view out into the garden. My mother looked very surprised, and when I asked her why, she said that my memory was spot on, but that I hadn't been born at the time of the event I described. It is not a scene that anyone ever had a reason to tell me about, or photograph, but it was a time of high emotion for her – the very conditions that we know allow information to become deeply installed in our subconscious minds.

As a therapist, I am aware that some behaviour patterns are much harder to shift than others. Maybe these are the inherited ones that are more deeply wired. I have some personal evidence for this – I have a fairly insignificant phobia that I share with my mother, and several different therapeutic attempts have failed to shift it. This theory would make sense because I would imagine that our true, anthropological instincts would be virtually impossible to change in the therapy room.

Cellular memory – the evidence from organ transplants

I promised earlier in the chapter to say a few words about this phenomenon. I have to admit that when I first heard about it I was sceptical, but there is a wealth of evidence from respected medical sources that this actually does happen. You only have to do a Google search for 'cellular memory' to find a wide range of sources which document an extraordinary variety of totally unrelated examples.

The claim made by many organ recipients is that after their transplant operations, some of their interests, tastes and memories changed – sometimes radically. For several medical and ethical reasons, organ recipients are not told any details of the donor of their organ except age and sex, so when their claimed changes turn out to match the characteristics of the donor which are only known to the medical staff, it is hard to ignore the evidence.

Let me give you an example which demonstrated a beautiful karmic justice. An eight-year-old girl received the heart of a ten-year-old girl who had been murdered. After the operation, she started having unexplained nightmares and her psychiatrist suspected that she was somehow re-experiencing the murder that had killed the donor. The police were called, and she was able to give enough information to them that they were able to identify and arrest the culprit. Confronted with her testimony, he confessed and admitted that her version of events described exactly what had happened.

The significance of this is hard to underestimate because if many or all of the cells in our bodies store memories and trapped emotions, it goes a long way to explaining how psychosomatic illnesses occur. This suggestion is fully in line with the theories which Dr Bruce Lipton expresses in his book *The Biology of Belief.*

This is another fascinating book which begins to make sense of the mind/body connection in credible, scientific terms.

Dr Bruce Lipton and *The Biology of Belief*

I have a logical mind which likes to know the science behind how things work. Despite what you might already be thinking, I am not very suggestible and do not take things at face value. I either want to understand the underlying processes, or I want to see some pretty strong evidence before I accept the truth of a new idea. Dr Lipton's book went a long way towards doing this for me in the area of how the mind and body are so inextricably linked.

Dr Lipton is a renowned cellular biologist, and the *The Biology of Belief* was the first book I read that explained the mind/body connection in practical terms that made sense to me.[7] He realised that cells are actually each like miniature microprocessors, changing their biochemistry in direct response to chemical and electrical signals in their environment. This implies, among many other things, that our thoughts can change the biochemistry of our cells for better or for worse. This in effect explains how the placebo effect works, and also how emotions that are 'trapped' in the body can cause illness. This observation also ties in with the emerging science of epigenetics, which postulates that environmental factors, including our thoughts, affect the way that our body 'interprets' our DNA.

When I read that there were fifty trillion cells in the human body, I immediately assumed that each individual cell must be pretty small and relatively simple. Small they might be, but simple they are definitely not. Each cell can have literally millions of receptors which receive messages from thousands of different hormones and neurotransmitters, and every message received can change the cell's biochemistry and behaviour. Crucially, some of the messages are electrical in nature which implies that there is a mechanism by which our thoughts can directly affect cell chemistry. The inevitable implication of his groundbreaking work is that our minds have much more control over our biochemistry and our health than was previously thought, and this can work for or against us depending on whether our thoughts are positive or negative. Among many other things, it demonstrates the mechanism which would allow the mind to manifest psychosomatic illnesses.

Chapter 3

Making sense of relationships

Why do so many people find it difficult or impossible to make relationships work?

I have already talked a lot about neuroses – those buttons that other people push that really make us react. People don't have to be close to us emotionally to push those buttons, but the closer they are, the more easily they can do it. Unless we are exceptionally touchy, we do not regularly react badly to strangers. If our partner says something uncomplimentary about us, it is much more hurtful than when a stranger does. So the closer people are, the more likely they are to be able to push our buttons. And it is also true that we are more likely to react badly to criticism from people we care about – their criticism frightens us because the implication is that they might withdraw their love.

There are two other reasons why we are more likely to behave badly in close relationships. Firstly, we are more likely to display subconsciously-driven behaviour to people we are familiar with because we are naturally less conscious in our dealings with them. Secondly, we often reserve our worst behaviour for the people who love us because we assume they will be more likely to forgive us. So it is basically only when we are in relationships

68

that our buttons get regularly pushed, and we are challenged to resolve our issues. Very often, this will be happening to both parties in the relationship, and one person's bad behaviour often triggers the other person to react with a similar lack of emotional maturity. However, when we are not in a close relationship, any bad behaviour which we do display is less likely to be challenged, and it usually has less worrying potential consequences because we don't have a partner to lose.

A quick look at Transactional Analysis

The behaviour described above is very easy to observe when you understand the basic theory of Transactional Analysis, as originated by Eric Berne.[8] This theory suggests that in all human interactions, we are either behaving as an Adult, a Parent or a Child. You do not have to be a parent to do this. Let's assume that two adults in a relationship are having a conversation. The man inadvertently says something a bit condescending that triggers the woman to feel stupid. Because she has a neurosis about this from childhood, it triggers the 'Child' in her to react. In other words, because she is running on a program that was installed in childhood, she reacts as she would have done at the age at which the neurosis was installed. She feels hurt, so her childish reaction might be to withdraw from him. He senses this, and because he has a neurosis about being unloved, he accuses her of being insular and uncaring. He is now definitely in Child mode too. If he had not had that neurosis, he could have opted to stay in 'Adult' mode, and tried to reassure her, but like her, he lacked the emotional maturity to calm the situation down. The net result is that they both end up in Child mode having a slanging match and achieving absolutely nothing.

It is worth mentioning at this point that there is nothing wrong with two adults being light-hearted and interacting in Child mode - as long as the children are 'playing nicely'. The people who we might notice flipping in and out of Child mode on a regular basis are of course teenagers, and this should not surprise us because they are literally transitioning from childhood to adulthood. The reason that the best adult relationships are generally between the most emotionally mature people is that they have few, if any, buttons to push, so they naturally spend the vast majority of their time in Adult mode. If one of them does occasionally slip into Child mode, the other is much more likely to move to 'Parent' mode and reassure them, so they are soon back to Adult mode themselves.

Why are we so often attracted to the same type of people, and to familiar situations?

This is a really important question. To understand why, we need to examine how the subconscious mind is attempting to help us. It is actually very simple. By definition, we must already know how to cope with events which we have already experienced. If we didn't know how to cope with them, we would be dead, so basic logic dictates that familiar experiences clearly pose less of a threat to our survival than unfamiliar ones. So your subconscious mind is programmed to attract you to familiar situations, and to people who behave in familiar ways, to supposedly make your life easier and safer.

In a perfect world, with loving and emotionally mature parents who were skilled at child-rearing, this would be a great strategy. However, if your childhood was less than ideal in this respect, you will quite possibly spend your life being attracted to people with similar shortcomings to those of your parents. It has long been recognised that women whose mothers were physically abused by their fathers are statistically much more likely to choose partners who will abuse them.[9] This makes no sense at all on the face of it – you would think that they would consciously go out of their way to avoid being subjected to the same appalling situation. But their attraction to abusive men is simply a consequence of their subconscious minds trying to help them. This particular feature of the subconscious mind can be very unhelpful indeed, causing a lifetime of troubled relationships and unhappiness.

A great example of this process in action

I heard an interview recently which demonstrated this perfectly.[10] It was with Hilary Devey, an entrepreneur who has been phenomenally successful in the haulage business. When she was fourteen, the family discovered that her father was a bigamist, and when this came to light her parents split up, although they later reunited. Years later, Hilary Devey met a guy she liked and settled down with him and had a child. One day the phone rang and it was a woman who claimed to be Hilary's partner's wife. It turned out to be true – Hilary had also been attracted to a man who was a bigamist. The statistical chances of this happening randomly are vanishingly small. It is an absolutely classic example of a person's subconscious mind attracting them to a person who would behave in a similar way to her own father. This provided her with a familiar situation, however much she may not have consciously wanted it. How did her subconscious mind 'read' the guy? I have absolutely no idea, but this so obviously happens that we are forced to accept that it is so. Hilary Devey split up with him, and has subsequently been married and divorced a further three times. She admits that she is good at judging men in business, but not in her personal life. In truth, it is simply that she does not understand how she has been programmed by her early life. Hilary – if you are reading this, the program can be uninstalled!

Case study – Sandra

Patterns like the one above are easy to identify, even if we don't understand the mechanism that allows them to happen. However, for some people, the source of their habitual patterns is much less obvious. Sandra was consistently drawn to men who treated her very badly, but her parents had had a loving and kind relationship. There was no obvious history of emotional abuse in her childhood that would explain her habitual attraction to men who would treat her so disrespectfully.

Under hypnosis, a very unusual story emerged which actually made perfect sense. From the age of nine, she had suffered considerable ill-health and abdominal pain. After three years of this she was rushed into hospital to have a large ovarian cyst removed. It turned out that the cyst, which was the size of a melon, was placed in a bucket where it burst and was seen to contain hair and teeth. Such cysts are known medically as fetiform teratomas. They are very rare, and are considered to occur where twins are conceived, and one foetus partially grows inside the other.

I have no idea what was actually said during the operation, but while in the trance state, Sandra had the very clear impression that she had effectively aborted her twin sister, and felt an immense sense of guilt that she had caused her twin to be discarded in a bucket as medical waste. In truth, it doesn't matter whether she was right or wrong – her emotion of guilt was generated by what she thought (subconsciously) to be the case.

It is worth mentioning at this point that during operations, anaesthesia does not put the subconscious to sleep – only the conscious mind is affected. There are many reports of hypnotised clients subsequently being able to repeat what has been said by surgeons during operations. Medical staff should always bear this fact in mind, and not say anything in front of an anaesthetised patient that they would not say if they were awake.

With Sandra still in the trance state, we reframed what had happened, and it then became obvious to her that she had absolutely nothing to reproach herself for. Once her thoughts on the matter changed, so did her emotions, and she felt so unburdened that she later told me that she had been singing loudly in the car on the way home from this session. She subsequently cut her ties with two married men who had been treating her badly, and she told me that, far from being drawn to them, she felt completely indifferent towards them from that time onwards.

Does this unhelpful subconscious programming have any other implications?

Yes – consistently being attracted to the wrong people is only one aspect of this tendency. The other implication of it is that we are all, completely unknowingly, sending messages to the subconscious minds of others, about what we are really like. The bigamist, the abuser, the player – they are all telling potential mates how they are likely to behave. If they weren't, the people programmed to be attracted to them couldn't find them. How this actually happens is a bit of a mystery, but it absolutely does happen. Body language is part of the story, but there must be much more to it than that. This might sound a bit wacky, but there is definite evidence that some kind of thought transmission between humans is not just possible, but almost certainly occurs. Rather than break the flow here, I have included a few words about this at the end of the chapter.

The good news here is that once you change your subconscious programs, you can use this 'messaging service' to avoid these people, rather than being attracted to them. But right now, what messages are you unknowingly putting out? For example, we have already discussed that by using kinesiology we can test and find out how few people genuinely love themselves at a deep, subconscious level. Sadly, it is probably a minority – so are the rest of us actually unknowingly signalling to the world that we are not worthy of being loved? We all know people who consistently make bad relationship choices – the clichés are the woman who always seeks out the 'bad boy', or the man who picks jealous women, one after another. I must confess that I have some experience in this area.

What I learned about my own programming

For years I genuinely believed that most women were on a spectrum that ranged from fairly irrational at one end to raving mad at the other. That was simply my experience of what my partners were usually like. I had no idea that the truth was very different – because of my life experiences, I was programmed to be attracted specifically to women who displayed covert signs of particular emotional issues. These issues were mainly of anger and jealousy, and my subconscious antennae never failed to pick them out.

When I was in my thirties and forties I knew a counsellor socially, and over a period of several years, I referred three of my girlfriends to her. She told me that, among the thousands of clients that she had worked with over many years, these were the three angriest clients she had ever encountered. You could assume from this that I had a special talent for making people very, very angry, but this was not true. My talent was for picking people who, on the face of it, seemed perfectly reasonable, but buried underneath that reasonable exterior was an intensity of anger that I found quite incomprehensible. For reasons that go back a long way, I have never liked being shouted at, so you can guess at the outcome of these relationships.

There is a sad irony here, because if your childhood was lacking in something, be it love, security, respect etc., it will have left you with a particular need for that thing in your relationships. But because of the way your subconscious mind works, it will attract you to exactly the wrong people to provide it – as we know, it constantly seeks that which is familiar. However, looking at the bigger picture, this is probably just as well because if you *feel* that somebody else makes you whole, you are never actually challenged to achieve personal growth and *become* whole.

To begin to learn about yourself, your neuroses and the fears that you learned in your childhood, you need to study your own behaviour and the behaviour of the partners you choose. What are the similarities between your partners? Are they often unavailable, unreliable or unfaithful? Are they often bullying, critical or sarcastic? What features and faults do they share with your parents? What buttons do they consistently press in you? Do not just look at the parent of the same sex as your partner. If either parent was an alcoholic for instance, children of both sexes will be more likely to be attracted to an alcoholic partner themselves. Ask a close friend to help you do this analysis – we sometimes struggle to see things about ourselves that are blindingly obvious to others.

There is some crossover here with the content of the previous chapter about core beliefs. If, for instance, you do not believe that you deserve to be treated with love and respect, you could spend your life being attracted to people who will not treat you with love and respect. Your subconscious mind is always attempting to achieve the outcomes in life which you expect, because what is familiar is perceived as less of a threat than what is unfamiliar.

Why do we even try to have relationships?

There is no question that human beings are programmed to live in couples – to have a 'mate'. We have physical and psychological adaptations which make this a sensible option. Touching, stroking, kissing and having sex with a partner flood the body with pleasurable hormones like oxytocin which increase bonding. I doubt if there is another animal on the planet that has such a strong and prolonged urge to indulge in non-procreative sex with a partner. Who was it that said, 'sex is like oxygen – it's no big deal unless you're not getting any'?

If you need any more convincing that human contact is crucially important to us, at all ages, consider the following:

1. If newborn babies are left untouched, in incubators for example, it soon makes a measurable difference to their development (physical weight, brain size, etc.) compared to babies in incubators who are touched often.

2. For prisoners, the ultimate punishment is solitary confinement, the use of which is generally regarded as inhumane.

3. Statistically, people in long-term relationships live longer, healthier and happier lives.

But if this is our natural state, why do some of us find it so hard to achieve harmonious relationships? Why is the divorce rate so high? Why do so many people give up and choose to live alone? Figures released in the UK by the Office for National Statistics in 2015 report that a staggering 51% of the adult population are single. I have mentioned this before, but it is an uncomfortable truth that if, like I did, you have a string of failed relationships behind you, they only have one common denominator – YOU. But as previously mentioned, if you give up and opt for a single life, it is likely to slow your emotional growth to a standstill as well as impair your physical health in the longer term.

What do we want from relationships?

The fundamental answer to this question for most people is that we want somebody who makes us feel good about ourselves. In truth of course, they are not *making* us feel good, but *allowing* us to. People allow us to feel good about ourselves by allaying the fears and insecurities that we have brought with us from childhood. For instance, if we fear that we are unlovable, we will feel much better living with someone who 'makes' us feel loved. If we lacked security in our childhood, we will feel safer with someone who offers that security. But in reality, these feelings of love and security are an illusion because, in the long run, no one can continually *make* us feel anything. Sooner or later our partner will do or say something that triggers us to question the feeling we were relying on, and we can rapidly panic.

The reason I say that no one can make us feel anything is actually very simple. Our feelings are generated by our thoughts, and this is a really important thing to understand. We often hear people say that they can't help how they feel, but this just isn't true. They simply have to choose a different thought to generate a different feeling. The whole cycle is as follows:

1. An external stimulus generates a thought. Let us suppose a tiger sticks its head around the door. The thought is – to keep it polite - 'oh no, I might get eaten!'
2. This generates an emotion, which in this case will almost certainly be fear. Emotions are also called feelings because we can feel a physical change in our bodies. What we are actually feeling in this case is the effects of

adrenaline being released – increased heart rate, blood pressure, etc. These changes are being made in our body to facilitate the next step...

3. Action! We need to fight or flee to avoid getting eaten, and we are now physically pumped up and ready to jump out of the window and escape the threat.

Once we have done this, and we see that we have put a safe distance between us and the tiger (new stimulus), we realise that we are now safe (new thought) and we feel elated as endorphins flood our body (new emotion), and we laugh (or cry) and leap up and down (new action).

There is a clear message here;

If you want to change the way you feel, change the way you think!

When I say that you cannot actually make, or even force, anyone to feel anything, here is another example. I would like you to try and envisage making the Dalai Lama angry. I suspect that this would be almost impossible to do. If you behaved in a way that you thought might make him angry, he would probably just be puzzled and would end up feeling sorry for you. This is because he probably doesn't have any repressed anger in him - the button isn't there to press. I am not saying that someone who is very emotionally mature could never feel angry, but people are much more likely to express emotions which they have not resolved within themselves. If a person was abused as a child, you could potentially expect them to express a lot of anger on a day-to-day basis. However, if a person had an idyllic childhood, he would be much, much less likely to ever lose his temper. Once you accept the truth of this and take complete responsibility for your own feelings, you have taken a huge step forward towards emotional maturity.

I have said this before, and I will say it again - the best relationships are between the most emotionally mature people – they don't press each other's buttons because they have few, if any, buttons to press. You will recall that in Chapter 1 I mentioned that the behavioural programs that we call neuroses are usually installed in childhood. For this reason, almost by definition, they involve childish behaviour. They cannot be otherwise because they are instinctive reactions to events which occurred in childhood and have not changed since you were that age. What you did then, you do now, when the same button is pushed.

I like to think of people as being like a set of Russian dolls. In a very real sense, although we get bigger as we get older, the small child of years ago is still within us, and is still very capable of expressing itself. Achieving emotional maturity is a matter of listening to that child and resolving its issues so that it is comforted, and current events no longer trigger fears that make it panic. When people 'push your buttons' and trigger behaviour that in hindsight you are not proud of, they have usually frightened your inner child. It is only by going back in time and listening to the fears of the inner child that we can make real progress. This is what 'inner child' work sets out to achieve, whether conducted consciously, or under hypnosis. When we do this, we become well placed to enjoy happy adult relationships because we simply no longer have buttons that can be pushed. The key attribute of emotionally mature people is that they always respond in an adult way when issues inevitably arise. It's a great place to be.

Why are relationships often so challenging?

We have already established that if we don't have close relationships, people can't easily hurt us – we have no expectations of them, so by definition, they cannot let us down. By letting people close, we allow them access to our buttons, and the pain and stress of having them pushed is no more and no less than a challenge for us to change. There is no question that we reserve our worst behaviour for the people we care about most – we assume that they are the most likely people to put up with it and forgive us for it. But to grow emotionally, we need to find a better strategy than to lash out when we feel pain. The pain is in fact a sign that we have a 'trapped emotion', and it presents an opportunity for us to identify and release it, and in doing so, move one step closer towards emotional maturity.

The real and permanent solution to this is explained in the last chapters of the book, but here is a good strategy until you get there if your partner presses a button. Promise yourself that you will not react in any way to anything that presses your buttons until twenty-four hours have passed. By doing this you are telling your inner child that you will let him have his say, but only when he has calmed down (this is not a bad policy with children generally!) Emotions are usually fairly transient, and the ensuing calm period gives you time to reflect on whether your instinctive reaction was justified (i.e. you really were wronged by someone), or whether your instinctive reaction may have been a bit unreasonable. If the latter is the case, you have learned something valuable about yourself.

If, after the cooling off period, you feel you were wronged and you wish to discuss the matter with your partner, do not tell them they were wrong, or criticise them. Simply say, 'When you did that (shouted, for example), I felt this (disrespected, humiliated, unloved, or whatever)'. You are not making any accusations, you are not criticising, you are not being confrontational – you are merely giving constructive feedback. If your partner loves you, they will care how you feel, and hopefully respond in a similarly mature way to try and resolve the issue.

There are many people who consider that trapped emotions do not just form the basis of neuroses – they are considered to be the root cause of many psychosomatic illnesses. Many books have been written on this subject, and I look at this subject in more detail in Chapter 6.

Why do new relationships seem to start off so well, but frequently end so badly?

Many people find this puzzling, but there is really no mystery about it. When you meet a new person and you are attracted to them, being with them allows you to feel good about yourself. Most of us know the amazing feeling of falling in love. Because it is so pleasurable, we are extremely aware of every minute we spend with our new lover – in other words we are extremely *conscious* in our interactions with that person.

But we are all programmed to delegate as many tasks as possible to the subconscious mind. This process is described in detail in Chapter 1 – we know that as soon as our subconscious mind recognises a familiar situation that it thinks it can apply a routine response to, it will do so. When the novelty of being with our new partner wears off, we begin to respond to them unthinkingly, and we display signs of our subconscious programs to them. These behaviours are rarely as attractive as the behaviours we have consciously been presenting to our partner up to that point. They could for example include being irritable or swearing, which most people would not do on a first date. But as time goes by, we revert to habitual behaviour as the novelty of the relationship gradually morphs into a part of our everyday life.

We have become complacent about giving our new partner the special treatment that we previously displayed. And of course, they are doing exactly the same thing to us at about the same point in time. We don't like it any more than they do – we think (correctly) that we are seeing another side to them that we didn't know existed. They are disappointing us, and not treating us with the love and respect that they previously displayed. They are, in fact, showing us that they are really no different to the previous lovers we have fallen out with because in a few months their behaviour changed out of all recognition - they went from being loving and attentive to belching at mealtimes and farting in bed.

How can we stop this happening?

The solution to this, in theory at least, is simple. When we meet new people, particularly people we are attracted to, we present our best side to them. But we can't keep this up forever. The more we like them, the more conscious we are in their company, and the longer our good behaviour lasts. But sooner or later the reality gap becomes apparent. The reality gap is the difference between the person we would like them to think we are, and the person who we really are.

The solution to this is to work on our subconscious programs so that when we slip into autopilot, our behaviour doesn't deteriorate! We still behave well and always respond to challenges in an adult manner. That is really what this whole book is about – becoming emotionally mature so that our automatic responses to people are always 'grown-up'. This is, of course, easier said than done, but it is perfectly achievable, and the rewards in peace of mind and quality of relationships are immeasurable.

Does it become harder to have new relationships as you get older?

There is some reason to think that this is so. As people gradually become more emotionally mature, their ability to have functioning relationships increases, so these fish leave the dating pool. Unfortunately, it therefore follows that the older members of that pool tend to have more serious issues which they have failed to resolve. This is of course only a general trend, and does not allow for people who suddenly become single again through no fault of their own.

I met a very glamorous elderly lady once who had had a very colourful romantic career. She had been married and divorced four times and had had numerous other affairs while both married and single. From memory, I think she had four children, and to the best of my knowledge none of them had the same father. Her explanation for why it became increasingly hard to find a suitable partner as you got older was that as you aged, two things happened – you simultaneously became more choosey and less attractive. She considered that these factors worked against each other so that the statistical chances of finding a decent partner reduced very rapidly as you aged. It is hard to argue with her logic!

How to improve your relationships generally – some practical ideas

Almost everyone I have ever asked has heard of the book *How to Win Friends and Influence People* by Dale Carnegie, but hardly any of them has ever actually read it.[11] It has now sold over thirty million copies and is rated by *Time Magazine* as one of the top twenty most influential books ever written. Given that its subject matter is one that affects us all every day of our lives, (unless you are unfortunate enough to be in solitary confinement), I can only suggest that you get a copy and read it. I did not realise until I had finished it that it was written over eighty years ago, but don't let this put you off because human nature doesn't change – the book is as current today as the day it was written.

You might wonder why we need to be taught how to get on with other people, but few people instinctively understand much about the psychology of human relations. With just a little knowledge, we can make massive improvements to the quality of our interactions with friends and strangers alike. For example, when most of us want somebody to like us, we try and impress them. We would have much more success if we did nothing of the sort. What we need to do is simply listen to them and let them impress us. If you do this, it makes them feel good about themselves, and they then enjoy spending time with you because they feel good when they do.

Likewise, if we want somebody to do something, we usually tell them what we want and why we want it. The problem with this is that fundamentally, other people often don't care what we want. If we thought a bit deeper and explained what the advantages to *them* would be if they did it, they would be likely to engage with us much more willingly. Dale Carnegie, the author, is truly a master of his subject, and the book is absolutely crammed with invaluable advice about getting on better with our fellow human beings.

If you want to step up another level, read *The Charisma Myth* by Olivia Fox Cabane.[12] This is another outstanding book, and the title reflects the fact that it is a myth that you are either born charismatic, or you are not. Fox Cabane analyses how the behaviour of highly charismatic people is different from that of others, and explains why they affect us the way they do in anthropological terms. Basically, if you were foraging ten thousand years ago, and you wandered away from your tribe and met a stranger, your survival could be at stake. You would need to analyse three things about them to assess whether you were in danger. Do they look powerful? Have they noticed you? And are they friendly or hostile? The worst-case scenario is that they look powerful, they have noticed you and they look hostile, because this makes them a potentially serious threat to you. The best-case scenario is that they look powerful, they have noticed you and they look friendly because this could make them a great ally. The implication is that they have power and influence, and they are predisposed to use it in your favour.

Fox Cabane therefore deduces that the three components of charismatic behaviour are power, presence and kindness. Any one of these qualities can make you charismatic to some extent, but if you can combine all three you are really onto a winner. To give examples, Barack Obama would be considered to have power-based charisma, Bill Clinton's is fundamentally presence-based and the Dalai Lama exudes kindness-based charisma. The book then explains in detail how each of these is achieved by the way we dress, our body language, eye contact, conversational techniques, and much, much more.

Some things are really easy to do, such as taking more care with how you dress and cleaning your shoes. For many thousands of years, tribal leaders and people in authority had better clothes than those they led, and today we still instinctively show more respect to well-dressed people. Historically, good shoes were particularly expensive, and we still notice them today as status symbols for that reason.

Much of Fox Cabane's advice is behavioural, such as never butting in when other people are speaking, waiting two seconds after they finish before you respond (to give the impression that you were so wrapped up in what they were saying that you had not thought about your response) and giving them appropriate, but not intimidating, eye contact. If some of these behaviours do not come naturally to you, her message is simple – 'fake it till you make it!' This advice ties in nicely with a message that runs right through this book – if you keep doing something consciously, your subconscious mind will soon recognise the repeating pattern of behaviour, and it becomes a habit. At that point, you will have increased your natural level of charisma.

Understanding why people do what they do

When Sigmund Freud began to study human nature, he pretty quickly noticed that behaviourally, people fell into various categories.[13] He gave them names such as Oral Receptive, Genital Hysteric and Anal Retentive because he thought that their personalities were determined by events that had occurred to them at key times in their young lives as they became aware of their mouth and other important parts of their anatomy! Most people would agree that they were not particularly attractive names, and as Freud's theory became widely discredited, psychologists preferred to call the categories Resolute Organisational, Intuitive Adaptable and Charismatic Evidential.

More recently still, Terence Watts' book *Warriors, Settlers and Nomads* offers a very credible explanation of these character types in anthropological terms.[14] It is a very interesting read, and it provides a simple but effective model for characterising people, and to some extent, predicting their behaviour. The characteristics of the three groups are as follows:

- Resolute Organisational, or *Warriors*: Organised, self-disciplined, natural leaders, hate to be seen to be wrong, not unduly concerned about what other people think about them, somewhat unforgiving, reliable and tenacious, apparently unemotional.

- Intuitive Adaptable, or *Settlers*: Definitely people-pleasers, very concerned about what other people think of them, dislike confrontation, very willing to compromise, very instinctive, often lacking in confidence.

- Charismatic Evidential, or *Nomads*: Outgoing, emotional, dramatic, need constant stimulation, very enthusiastic but easily bored, a tendency to exaggerate and be boastful, fun-loving party animals, and tendency to be late or unreliable.

Terence Watts suggests that most people actually display characteristics of all three types, but in different proportions – some people's characteristics clearly fall strongly into one group, and others display a more evenly balanced mix. He offers a multiple-choice kit for quickly determining the proportions of each personality type for any specific person. Being able to easily and accurately determine a client's personality type has specific benefits for the therapist, but it is also a great skill to have in everyday life for several reasons:

1. It increases your self-awareness, and allows you, for example, to choose a job which suits your instinctive behaviour. If you are a Warrior, running your own business might suit you better than being a small cog in

a big business machine where you are constantly accountable to other people. If you are a Nomad, being a salesman is likely to suit you better than working on your own or being an accountant.

2. It helps you to understand others, and to be more tolerant of their behaviour, particularly when it is vastly different from your own. If you have a friend who is great fun and makes you laugh a lot, but is sometimes late and unreliable, you will understand that the two things can't be separated. They are functions of each other. If you have children whose behaviour is wildly different from your own, it could save both you and them a lot of stress because it might give you the wisdom not to try to mould them in your image – a task which is doomed to fail.

3. If you employ people, it is enormously helpful in recruiting the right *type* of person for a specific job. If you have ever employed a very well qualified person to a post and it just didn't work out, it could well have been because they were the wrong *type* of person for the job. To thrive in a job, a person needs the right skills *and* the right attitude. Don't put a Warrior on the customer relations team – it is likely to end in tears (yours and your customers')! At the end of the day, you can teach people the skills you need them to have, but you can't change

their attitude to any great extent. So using personality analysis is a very useful tool for the potential employer.

Can we read each other's thoughts?

There is growing scientific evidence for this, but little understanding of how it could work. I said in Chapter 1 that I instinctively much prefer to understand how things work if I am going to believe in them, but during the research for this book I came to realise that this is actually not always a very sensible attitude. For example, I do not begin to understand how the computer that I am currently using works, but I can't deny that it does work. So, let's accept that we don't know how this works, and just look at the evidence.

Here are a couple of examples of thought reading that you might be able to relate to.

Firstly, there are a significant number of people who sometimes feel that they know who is calling them on the phone without looking at the caller ID. Controlled experiments have been conducted where four people were randomly asked to ring the test subject during the day, and the test subject had to guess who was calling before they answered the phone. Statistically, you would expect them to be right 25% of the time. The people best at doing this regularly beat the statistical odds of doing this by a factor of two – in other words, they were right 50% of the time.

When I read this, it made me recall something my grandfather had told me when I was a child. His brother Jake had emigrated to Canada, and because transatlantic phone calls were extremely expensive at the time, they only spoke about once a year, at totally random times. On one occasion he felt it was time to ring his brother, so he picked up the phone to make the call. Imagine his astonishment when his brother was actually there, on the line, without him dialling! Jake had also had the urge to call his brother just a few seconds before, and my grandfather had picked up the phone before it had a chance to ring.

Secondly, a lot of people claim to be able to sense when people behind them are looking at them. This concept is accepted to such a degree that when the security services teach operatives how to undertake covert surveillance – i.e. how to follow a suspect without being observed - they instruct them never to stare directly at the back of the suspect's head. They teach the operative to look past the suspect, and keep them in their peripheral vision, not their direct sight.

What is considerably more bizarre is anecdotal evidence that comes from people whose job it is to man the CCTV screens at security centres for places such as shopping centres. They claim that it is quite often possible to make a complete stranger turn around and look in the general direction of the camera, just by staring at the back of their head on the screen, even when the security monitoring centre is geographically miles away from the shopping centre.

Many closely-related people, or people in close relationships, report frequently thinking about the same thing at the same time. I have done this on many occasions. It is widely reported that more 'primitive' societies, from the Kalahari Bushmen to the Australian Aborigines, can communicate telepathically, even over great distances.[15] This could make sense if the reason that we lost the ability to do this was that, as our civilisation became more sophisticated, we were forced to turn to language to communicate increasingly complex thoughts. If a group of Bushmen were out hunting, they might want to communicate to their village the message 'we have made a kill' (so light the fire!) – fairly simple.

In today's world, telepathically communicating 'I haven't yet finished the report that I have to present to the board in the morning, and the train drivers have gone on strike, so I won't be home before 10pm' would be considerably trickier.

I once heard a striking - and very sad - example of thought transference. It related to a young girl who was virtually blind, and her mother regularly took her to an eye specialist to try and find out the cause. On each visit, the young girl sat with her mother as she tried to identify simple shapes and colours on cards that the specialist held up. She was often able to do this, but one day her mother had to leave the room, and the specialist noticed that the girl couldn't give a single correct answer in her mother's absence. It turned out that this was not a matter of confidence – the girl still couldn't actually see even if her mother was present, but was not looking at the cards. The inevitable conclusion was that she was in fact blind, but had formed such a close, dependent bond with her mother that she could read her mother's thoughts.

Chapter 4

The hidden programs that determine our behaviour

The difference between having neuroses and being neurotic

Another feature of our subconscious mind that is highly relevant to our behaviour is that in childhood it picks up 'programs' which can dictate our behaviour throughout our lives. These programs are often very simple, and just consist of 'when 'x' happens, do 'y'. They are much like the stimulus-response programs that affect our relationships, but they affect things like our general behaviour and our response to stress.

Have you ever looked back at the way you behaved in a particular situation, and really not understood why you did what you did? Have you realised that it was not in your best interests to behave that way, and made a resolution not to repeat it? And have you then gone and done exactly the same thing the next time, like a moth drawn to a candle flame? We all do this, because we are all running on subconsciously held behavioural programs that we are, by definition, unaware of.

These programs could loosely be described as neuroses. Having a neurosis is not the same as being neurotic. We all have neuroses of some type or another. These manifest themselves in our daily lives by triggering us to behave in ways that are not, in emotional terms, completely predictable and 'normal'. We are usually aware of them, but think they are 'just the way we are'. They are the buttons that are triggered by various situations, and cause us to react in ways that others may not. The truth is that, while I think it is possible that some people are born with those buttons already in place, for most people it is not the case. From my experience as a therapist, I know that most people's neuroses can definitely be traced back to events in their lives, mostly in childhood.

Being neurotic is something different. A neurotic person has a continual level of anxiety, and as a result they find it extremely hard to relax. In this context, I would define anxiety as 'non-specific fear'. I suspect that some neurotic behaviour can be learned from our parents. However, like most neuroses, it can also often be traced back to a specific traumatic event. This is pure conjecture, but I wonder if being neurotic is possibly more common in women than men for anthropological reasons. We all have the choice whether to fight or flee when our survival is threatened. It makes sense that men who are typically stronger and more aggressive than women would be more likely to choose to fight. Being more confrontational, they are more likely to address the issues that stress them. By the same logic, women are less likely to do so, and consequently, remain fearful because in the modern world we often cannot just run away from the issues that cause us stress.

As a matter of interest, when people talk about the fight or flight response, that is slightly simplistic. There are actually three instinctive 'F's when we perceive a serious threat. The first is freeze, and during this phase we assess whether the threat - let us say a tiger again - has seen us or not. If it has not, staying absolutely still may well be our best option, and this can take the form of a temporary paralysis. It is only if the tiger has seen us that we need to choose fight or flight. When people describe themselves as being so frightened that they were 'rooted to the spot', they are simply unable to break out of this instinct to stay still. An extreme example of this behaviour is seen in fainting, or myotonic, goats. They have a genetic anomaly which prolongs the 'freeze' instinct for about five to twenty seconds, and frequently makes them go completely rigid and sometimes fall over when startled. There are some very amusing videos on the internet demonstrating this.

Back to neuroses. Neurotic people are often said to live on their nerves, and because it takes libidic energy to hold each repression in place, their libido is frequently low or non-existent. However, the fact that they are 'uptight' does not in any way imply that jovial or humorous people are free from neuroses – sometimes humour can be a cover strategy for severe emotional discomfort. Think Robin Williams or Spike Milligan.

Case study – John

Last year a young man contacted me to help him because his anxiety levels really were off the scale. The list of things he was scared of included women, driving, the dark, eating out and many others. In fact, his life consisted of doing a solitary job, and then going back to his room in his parent's house. He hardly ever went out other than to work.

Under hypnosis, he recounted a story which immediately revealed the source of his problems. When he was eight, his parents had an argument, and his mother took a piece of rope and said she was going out into the garden to hang herself. He was obviously terrified and asked his Dad to stop her. His Dad's reply was, 'Oh, don't worry – I think she's just being dramatic – I don't suppose she will go through with it. Let's go and watch telly'. So this little boy was forced to watch TV while he thought his mother was actually hanging herself in the garden. He was being prevented from expressing the very real terror that he felt, and the emotion was *repressed* rather than being *expressed*. His mother did not hang herself, but that did not prevent the experience from scarring him deeply.

When he recounted this story under hypnosis he was very tearful, and when he finished I asked him to tell it to me again. On the second and third tellings he gave successively more detail, but less emotion. By the fourth time, John could recount the story without any emotion at all. At this point, I knew that the repression was fully released. When he arrived for his session the following week, he had driven himself, in the dark, and he had joined a gym. A few months later, I heard that he had moved out from his parents' house, had bought a flat and his first girlfriend was living with him. He really was a changed man. In truth, he was much closer to being the man he would have been had he not suffered that appalling experience as a young boy.

An example of being neurotic

I met a lady quite recently who was not a client - she was a friend of a friend. She was, without doubt, one of the most neurotic people I have ever met. Her continual anxiety was absolutely obvious to me from the moment we met - in her posture, her language patterns, her facial expressions and her body language. When she learned that I was a therapist, the conversation eventually turned to this issue. I told her there was almost certainly an event in her past that had triggered her anxiety, but she flatly denied this. She told me she had had an idyllic childhood and felt loved and cared for at all times.

Then she mentioned, almost in passing, that when she was ten, her grandfather had been shot dead in an underworld killing! The sudden death of someone we care about is always a shock, but the nature of that death makes a huge difference to how we cope with it. If he had died of old age, or a heart attack, it would not have implied any personal danger to her. But as far as her impressionable ten-year-old subconscious mind was concerned, if he could get blown away, so could she.

I explained in Chapter 1 that we are especially vulnerable to installing subconscious programs at times of high emotion, and the manner of her grandfather's death was absolutely terrifying. At that young age, she would have been very suggestible as well, and the outcome does not surprise me at all.

Sometimes, these programs that we inadvertently pick up only affect specific areas of our lives, and we can live with them. For instance, if you were regularly criticised as a child, you may well have become defensive. While this is not a great characteristic to have, it only affects you as an adult when people criticise you, and that may not be very often. However, other types of program could potentially have a huge impact on our lives, and I would like to give you an example of this from my own life that demonstrates this clearly. The behaviour pattern it triggered caused a massive amount of stress and unhappiness, and nearly got me killed more than once.

My chaotic life – before I eventually understood my own faulty programming

The number of times in my life I have done things that could have ended disastrously is quite unbelievable. Here is a sample of the activities and occurrences that gave my Mum more than a few grey hairs.

As a child, from about ten onwards, I was fascinated by fire and explosives. Apart from nearly burning our house down, I regularly used to blow things up, and on at least two occasions, was very lucky not to be seriously injured or killed.

I once built a gas furnace from a few bits of steel pipe and the motor from a vacuum cleaner. To try it out, I heated up a large flint to about 700 degrees Celsius, at which point the stone blew up right in front of my face. How all the bits missed me I will never know to this day.

I have very nearly drowned three times in my life - on one occasion as a small boy I dived to the bottom of a swimming pool and pushed my finger through a grill - and got it stuck.

On my honeymoon, I foolishly decided to go sightseeing on a glacier. If I could have read the signs in German which said: 'Beware avalanches and crevasses', I might have known what was about to happen. The crevasse I chose to walk over was hundreds of feet deep and had a thin skin of wind-blown snow concealing it from the casual observer. I strolled along without a care in the world until the snow gave way underneath me without warning. Few people have lived to describe this type of experience.

Falling out of trees should never happen to a tree surgeon. It has happened to me three times - on the first occasion I was unconscious for several hours and woke up inside a brain scanner.

I suffered a very high-speed crash while skiing in Italy. I was probably going at about 70mph when one of my skis came off, the tip dug in the snow and then flicked up behind me and hit me in the back of the head. It all happened so fast that I had no idea what had actually occurred, but I was instantly knocked unconscious. I woke up with my head in a snow drift hundreds of metres further down the mountain. This was one of many times in my life when I have been completely knocked out.

I used to do karate, until I sustained a back injury that, after years of crippling pain, ultimately required five hours of spinal surgery to resolve.

In my early twenties I fell asleep at the wheel coming down a steep hill and woke up to a sudden bang as the car was launched into the air and hurtled down a motorway embankment.

In my thirties, I crashed a Land Rover and trailer on the M25, wrecking all the kit, but walking away unharmed.

The list goes on and on - this is genuinely just a sample.

Despite clearly being 'accident prone', I chose to spend my working life as a tree surgeon - a very dangerous job which involves abseiling with chainsaws. I had numerous near-misses at work, including on one occasion cutting the top out of a large tree while I was still roped into it. And, as if doing a dangerous job were not enough, I spent my spare time doing adventure sports. I owned a powerful motorbike which I rode around various race circuits, including the Isle of Man TT on 'Mad Sunday' and I even went to Germany several times to ride a few laps of the famously dangerous Nürburgring. I also went paragliding, parachuting, scuba diving, off-piste skiing, potholing, cave-diving and bungee jumping.

This type of life is not 'normal', but I never questioned it because it felt normal to me. For nearly forty years, it never occurred to me that I might have become programmed to make life choices which made serious accidents and near-misses not just likely, but almost inevitable.

My light bulb moment - how I eventually worked out what was going wrong in my life

Understanding what was happening was a massive turning point for me – this is how it happened.

In June 2015, I was invited to speak at a conference in the Midlands, and as I drove up the fast lane of the M1, I was daydreaming. Most people do this on boring car journeys, driving on autopilot and letting their minds wander. Many people don't realise it, but this is actually a state of hypnosis. I daydreamed about having a tyre blow out, and crashing spectacularly, rolling the car a few times just for the dramatic effect. But, as with all my other catastrophic daydreams, I survived unharmed and walked away. On this occasion, I suddenly wondered why my daydreams often followed this theme, because they almost always did.

When I got to my hotel, I checked in and had an hour to spare before it was time to eat. I value time away from home because I invariably find it easier to see the 'bigger picture' without the distractions of my home environment. Almost all of the big decisions I have made in my life have been taken miles from home, and the revelation I was about to have was probably the most significant of my life. I thought about my car crash daydream again. I knew that hypnosis provides a window to the workings of the subconscious mind, and given that daydreams occur in a hypnotic state, there was obviously a deep significance to the fact that I kept doing this.

The catastrophic daydreams mirrored the reality of my life. In a very real sense, we create what we imagine. Maybe I was using the enormous power of my subconscious mind to visualise catastrophic events, and in doing so I was programming myself to be attracted to situations in life that could end badly. I knew enough about psychology to know that this made sense, but why on earth would I do it? What possible advantage could there be?

And then it dawned on me. As a child, I felt unloved. In truth I wasn't, but my parents weren't very demonstrative, and as I have already said, it isn't what happens to you in life that matters, it is what you *think* about what happens to you. Looking back at my childhood, there were a few occasions where I got physically hurt quite badly - because I led a boisterous outdoor life - and when I did, I received a lot of sympathy. I remember falling down a steep inland cliff in shorts and a T-shirt, and being battered and bruised, and absolutely lacerated by brambles. There wasn't a square inch of skin that wasn't scratched, bleeding or pricked with thorns. I was clearly in pain, and the ensuing sympathy felt particularly good to me because it *implied* that I was loved. In my mind, sympathy and love had become one and the same. Or at least sympathy had become a substitute for love that I ached to receive.

So if you naturally feel unloved and unlovable, creating situations that generate sympathy gives temporary relief to the emotional pain. I had inadvertently become programmed to be attracted to situations that were likely to go wrong, because the ensuing sympathy felt good. Unbeknown to me, my subconscious mind was actually looking for these situations to fulfil the subconscious desire to attract sympathy because I had learned that it was the only available substitute for love. And it did a good job!

Making sense of your past in order to understand your current subconscious programming is like doing a jigsaw when you haven't got the photo on the lid of the box. You are trying to create a picture without knowing what it looks like. But daydreams, sleeping dreams, recurring patterns of illness and hypnosis all offer a window into the subconscious, so we can glimpse pieces of the picture.

Another piece of the jigsaw falls into place

You might think that my adrenaline-fuelled leisure activities were simply an extension of this behaviour, but there is more to it than that. Because of a few thoughtless comments that were made to

110

me in my childhood, I grew up believing that I was cowardly, and also that other people thought I was too. So by consistently choosing to indulge in dangerous hobbies, I was demonstrating to everyone, including me, that this was not the case. By having a few accidents along the way, I was also generating sympathy, so there was a double pay-off. It was all beginning to make sense. Sitting on the bed in that hotel room, I suddenly realised that I had single-handedly generated the trail of disasters that littered my life up until that point.

My first step in turning this around was to be much more aware of my daydreams, and to instantly stop any that were heading for disastrous outcomes. I deliberately replaced them with positive outcomes where I felt loved and had no desire for sympathy. If you do anything routinely, your subconscious mind notices the pattern, and changes accordingly, taking over the routine. On the rare occasions that disastrous daydreams start to come to mind now, I spot them instantly and change the story completely.

How dreams can give us insight into the issues that trouble us

Our sleeping dreams also provide windows into the workings of our subconscious minds. For many years, I had a horrible nightmare where I was dazzled by a bright light and became permanently blind. Sometimes I would remember the nightmare when I awoke, but many other times I woke up feeling unaccountably worried by some unspecified fear. I realised years later that I had simply been repeatedly experiencing the same nightmare, without remembering it.

After many years of this, and about fifteen years ago, I went to an osteopath for some back treatment, and I mentioned this nightmare to him. He asked me if I knew why I had it. I explained that although there was nothing wrong with my sight, I was easily dazzled by bright lights. After examining me briefly, he asked me if I had ever had any serious impacts on the back of my neck. 'Quite a few as it happens,' was my honest answer. He explained that the nerves which control the movements of your eye and pupil dilation, actually enter the brain from the neck, and mine were so encased in scar tissue that they just didn't work very well. The interesting point here is that as soon as I understood *why* bright lights dazzled me, I never had that nightmare again – not even once. My subconscious mind had been trying, again and again, to understand the issue, and once it could make sense of the symptoms, the issue was resolved. So noticing your repeating dreams, or more specifically your repeating nightmares, or nightmares with repeating themes, offers another window into your subconscious.

Dreams and their interpretation

If you think this subject is a bit Freudian, please bear with me. Sigmund Freud had some strange ideas because he really was breaking new ground, and his theories concerned a new subject that was, by definition, highly theoretical. This made some of his ideas virtually impossible to test, and in some cases it has taken years to unearth evidence that either supports or undermines them. One area that I think he was right about was his suggestion that dreams are a method by which the subconscious mind attempts to solve problems. We know that the subconscious relates well to metaphors and analogies because that is the basis of most hypnotic scripts, and they clearly get their message across. To give you a practical example of the subconscious mind understanding metaphors, think about the stories we tell our children, like the *Tortoise and the Hare* from Aesop's Fables. A good storyteller en-*trances* (i.e. hypnotises) his audience, and in doing so, allows the metaphorical meaning of the story to enter the child's subconscious. It is an enjoyable way for us to teach our children many important lessons and morals of life. I suppose you could also call it brainwashing!

What I did not know about dreams until I read Dr Judith Orloff's book *Emotional Freedom*, is that if you want to access the intuitive wisdom of your subconscious mind, you can 'order' dreams on specific issues.[16] If this sounds a bit bonkers to you, I have to admit I had the same reaction myself when I read it. As a person who never remembers their dreams anyway unless I am suddenly awoken in the middle of them, I thought this was extremely unlikely to work for me. As I have hinted before, I am by nature sceptical, but I am also open-minded enough to give most things a chance. Here's what happened.

First the background. A while ago, I had three very serious issues weighing me down, and I honestly didn't know what to do about any of them, or what their eventual outcome would be. I am not by nature a worrier, but it would be an understatement to say that I had a lot on my plate. When I went to bed after reading that it was possible to order dreams, I set the intention to get some perspective on my situation. In the morning, I woke up from a dream where I was a traffic policeman who had been called to the scene of a road accident which had happened in the night. It was just getting light as I arrived at the scene to find three badly smashed cars set some distance apart from each other. I conducted a quick triage and chose the most damaged car to see if the driver had survived. When I approached the vehicle, there was no one in it, which was puzzling. Then I noticed a large box a few feet from the car and out of curiosity, I opened the lid. There was a woman in the box who had clearly been asleep, and she told me that after she crashed during the night she climbed in the box to sleep until it was light because she didn't know where she was.

The message I took from this dream was that even my worst problem would turn out well, and that if I could not immediately see the solution, it didn't matter. All would be revealed in time – I just needed to wait. This turned out to be true – all three of the problems eventually turned out well. I really was astonished at how well the dream ordering process had worked, and I have done it since with other issues that I wanted some clarity on.

Dr Orloff explains that there are essentially three different types of dream – psychological, predictive and guidance – and more importantly, she explains how to interpret them. As you wake up, try not to move, and stay in the dozy, hypnagogic state as long as possible. Keep the dream in mind, and let the interpretation come to you – don't try and force it.

Dr Orloff describes herself as an 'Energy Psychiatrist', and she asserts that all words and intentions have either a positive or a negative energy to them. While this sounds a bit 'out there', I have noticed that the few people who never swear or speak ill of anyone else, have an almost tangible aura of kindness and positive energy about them. One such person was my maternal grandfather, to whom this book is dedicated. He was absolutely not a pushover, but I never heard him speak ill of anybody, or anything, and he was one of the loveliest human beings you could ever hope to meet.

Can dreams make you really, chronically stressed?

About ten years ago, I came to realise that I really was chronically stressed. I had a resting heart rate which was well into the eighties, and I was snappy and intolerant. You might wonder why I didn't realise this before, but if you are always like it, it becomes your normality. You can only see that your behaviour was unreasonable on reflection, once you have calmed down. But if you never calm down, you can never see it.

Anyway, enough people told me that I was snappy that I realised that I had to sort the problem out. Thinking that my high pulse rate was probably an indicator of stress, and was certainly easy to measure, I bought a heart rate monitor and recorded the readings morning, noon and night. To my surprise, a pattern soon emerged which indicated that I was most stressed when I woke up, and that I gradually relaxed during the day. On the face of it, this seemed really odd – how could sleeping be stressful? Then I remembered the nightmares about being dazzled, and it occurred to me that it was just possible that I was having regular nightmares that I wasn't remembering. As I have previously explained, the subconscious mind generates physiological responses to imaginary events because it does not 'know' that they are not happening.

I contacted a dream therapist to see if she could help me to make sense of what I had noticed, but she told me that I would be better off seeing a hypno-analyst. I had never heard of hypno-analysis, but it was the best advice I ever received.

I searched out a hypno-analyst and explained the observations I had made. He said that he thought it very likely that my suspicions were correct, and that at night, my subconscious mind was regularly struggling to make sense of things that occurred in my distant past, without success. He told me that if I visited him once a week for an hour, he thought that we could resolve the problem in a couple of months or so. He predicted that after about two weeks I would start having much more dramatic dreams that I would remember, and when I stopped having these dreams the issue would be resolved. During the third week, I started having cataclysmic dreams involving tidal waves and buildings collapsing. I couldn't make sense of any of them, but the therapy had obviously started processing some issues buried deep in my subconscious mind.

The therapeutic process panned out exactly as my hypno-analyst had predicted, and after eight sessions he told me that he considered that the process was complete. I felt calmer than I ever remembered feeling. I felt a sense of lightness, as if some invisible weight had been lifted off me that I did not know I had been carrying.

To make sure that any change was not some kind of internal illusion, I had not told my partner that I was in therapy at all. At the end of the process I asked her if she had noticed any change in me. She had been my closest friend, but not my partner, for the last seventeen years, and my partner for the last two. She told me that she had never, ever seen me so calm. It is a calmness that has not just stayed with me, but it has deepened over time – partly as a result of other therapies that I have tried. A few months after I finished the course of hypno-analysis, somebody who I had met about a week previously said to me that I was the most laid-back guy he had ever come across. Few compliments have ever touched me so deeply – I had very clearly made a profound and lasting change for the better.

Hypno-analysis - a deepening interest, and new career path

In my early fifties I realised that while teaching tree climbing might be fun, it was not a career that I could expect to continue much longer. Over the years I had developed an interest in psychology in general, and therapy in particular, and began the process of re-training as a hypno-analyst myself. In the process of becoming a therapist, I had to undergo what is known as training analysis, which was my second and final experience of being on the hypno-analyst's couch. The purpose of training analysis is to go even deeper into the subconscious mind of the would-be therapist, and clear out any possible neuroses, or unwanted programs from the past, so that there are no buttons left to press. This is important for a therapist, because it is essential that any issues that clients raise in the therapy room leave the therapist emotionally unmoved. This doesn't mean that they don't care about their client – it simply means that the problems and experiences the client describes do not upset the therapist in any way.

I examine hypno-analysis in depth in Chapter 8 – it is, in my view, and in the view of most people who understand it, the cream of therapies. It seeks out, identifies and detoxifies each and every experience and misunderstanding that you have ever experienced in your life. At the end of the process I felt much happier in my own skin and much better equipped to enjoy excellent relationships than I had ever done before.

Chapter 5

Self-love and self-forgiveness

Why is self-love so important?

Most people are familiar with the Biblical quote 'Love thy neighbour as thyself'. There is a clear implication here that it is normal to love yourself at least as much as you love others, but how many of us do this? A lot of people struggle with the concept of self-love because they confuse it with being immodest at best, and egotistical at worst. For some people, even liking themselves seems difficult to achieve. However, the truth is that if you can learn to love yourself, it makes you modest – it is the people who are unhappy in their own skin who are tempted to 'big themselves up' and come across as boastful or egotistical. Also, people who don't like themselves are often tempted to be critical of others to make themselves feel better by comparison, and this trait will definitely not make you popular. And another thing - if you don't love yourself, how can you expect anyone else to?

So how do you do it? If you have a tendency to be kinder, more charitable and more forgiving to other people than you are to yourself, ask yourself why. Why do you single yourself out for harsher, less forgiving treatment? If you do something that you are not proud of, visualise having a conversation with yourself where you ask why it happened, learn the lessons for the future, then let it go. Learn how to forgive yourself. This is what you would do with anyone else, so why not be as forgiving with yourself? I have already talked about the power of visualisation – it is perfectly possible to visualise standing in front of another 'version' of you, and thereby have a conversation with yourself. You can do this looking back in time, so you are talking to the child that is actually within you, or with your adult self.

Also, when you get something right, take the time to praise yourself. Recognise your success, and don't just pass it off as 'normal', or just what you expect of yourself. Some people set such unrealistically high expectations of themselves that they inevitably fall short, and then they give themselves a hard time when they fail to meet their own unachievable standards. Looked at objectively, this makes absolutely no sense. Just be kinder to yourself.

When you understand what is involved in holding a grudge, failing to forgive others makes no sense at all, but failing to forgive yourself is even worse. Holding a grudge against someone has been compared to carrying a heavy rock around in the hope that you might get a chance to throw it at them. Usually, you don't even get the chance, so you just wear yourself out until you give up and drop the rock. How utterly pointless!

If you can find it in your heart to genuinely forgive someone at the time they hurt or offended you, you save yourself a lot of effort, and you like yourself more for being able to do it.

With regard to personal forgiveness, you are of course carrying the rock around with the intention of throwing it at yourself. Guilt is an indicator that you are not good at forgiving yourself. So, if you have a tendency to feel guilty, stand back and take a good look at *why* you do this. From my experience, I find that women are more likely to have this tendency than men. If you were unlucky enough to have had a parent who used guilt to manipulate you into complying with their wishes, it is likely that other people will trigger you to feel guilty as an adult. It is very much a tendency that is 'programmed in' at a young age, and it may need the help of a therapist to release it. More about this later.

Why are we often so self-critical?

As children, we are taught not to be immodest, but our childish minds can very easily fail to grasp subtle lessons. In the minds of most adults, there is a fine line between on the one hand having self-respect, self-confidence, taking pride in one's appearance and generally feeling good and positive about oneself, and on the other hand being proud, vain, boastful and egotistical. When adults see behaviour in their children which seems immodest in any way, parents generally jump on the behaviour because they don't want their child to grow up boastful or too 'full of themselves'. This is confusing for children because if, for example, they think they have drawn a great picture, it seems natural to say, 'Look Mummy, I have drawn a great picture'! If they immediately get put down, children quickly learn that thinking or saying positive things about themselves is somehow wrong.

As parents, in an attempt to stop them being immodest, we can very easily end up destroying all their positive instincts about themselves. Not only is this profoundly damaging to them, it is actually counterproductive. If we succeed in bringing up a child who feels good about themselves, they are far more likely to be modest than one who feels bad about themselves and ends us boasting in a sad attempt to make themselves feel better.

It is not unusual for modern parents to overcompensate for the poor parenting they received, and swing the pendulum too far the other way. In my opinion, it is at least as damaging as being too critical to constantly lavish praise on children for very mediocre performances. It is not rocket science – we need to praise them when they do well and give them help and guidance when they do not. When we inevitably need to criticise, it is essential to do it in a non-personal way. By this, I mean that you say, 'You did something bad', rather than, 'You ARE bad'. In any case, we can't undo the way we were spoken to as children, but we can unlearn the lessons that our childhoods left with us, and move on. We can certainly make sure that we speak to our own children or grandchildren with greater care and respect.

How do you improve your 'self-talk'?

It is very common for people to be much more aware of their shortcomings than they are of their successes. Visualise this scenario: you have got everything right, all day, and then you make one silly mistake and you say to yourself 'God, I'm so stupid!' Why do we engage in this negative self-talk? When we get things right we don't say 'God, I'm so clever!' (well most people don't, anyway). What is really puzzling about this is that we often personalise it – we don't say 'I *did* something stupid', we say 'I *am* stupid', so we are actually putting a very uncomplimentary label on ourselves. If we keep repeating it like a mantra throughout our lives, the belief just gets stronger and stronger. And as we now recognise, if you believe something at a deep level, your subconscious mind will ensure that you behave that way to fulfil your expectation that you will do stupid things.

There was probably a biological advantage to the tendency to be self-critical deep in our past. We definitely needed to be aware of our shortcomings because they might get us killed, whereas what we were good at did not threaten our survival. However, in today's world, this tendency does us far more harm than good, because if we repeat negative images of ourselves regularly enough, we eventually re-program our minds to that belief at a deeper level. This then becomes a self-fulfilling prophesy because we begin to unconsciously act the way we see ourselves.

There are several things we can do about this.

1. Make an effort to recognise when you get things right, and give yourself a pat on the back. We all recognise the benefits of complimenting our friends when they deserve it – why would we not do the same thing to ourselves?

2. Be prepared to recognise your own shortcomings, but do not 'personalise' them or see them out of context or perspective. If we are tired, or are learning a new skill, it is natural to make mistakes. Do not give yourself a hard time because of it.

3. Monitor your 'self-talk' all the time. Stop it immediately if it becomes negative. You can put a positive spin on just about anything. And because we now know that our thoughts determine our feelings, if we *think* more positively about ourselves, we will *feel* more positively about ourselves.

Compliments and criticism

Another strange habit that a lot of people have is to really take criticism to heart, but to shrug off compliments. When someone pays you a compliment, just accept it – you only have to say 'Thank you'. You can say more if you want, but you don't need to. If, instead of this, you mutter 'Oh, it was nothing', or something equally self-effacing, you don't feel the benefit of the compliment, and the person who gave it will probably think twice before paying you another one.

If on the other hand you are being criticised, try and work out the intention of the person delivering the criticism. If it is kindly meant as constructive negative feedback, it will be kindly said – listen to it and judge whether it can help you or not. By contrast, harsh criticism almost always says far more about the person making it - and their shortcomings - than it ever does about you. People who have low self esteem often criticise others for no better reason than to make themselves feel better by running you down. With a little practice you can spot this a mile off and totally disregard it.

How does our relationship with our parents affect us now?

Clearly, unhappy or painful experiences we had during childhood can have long-term adverse effects on our health and happiness as adults, but it really isn't helpful to blame our parents for this.

Indeed, the relationships we currently have with our parents continue to affect the way we relate to other adults in our lives. Your present relationship with your opposite sex parent will almost inevitably colour your relationship with your partner (or of course the same sex parent if you are in a same sex relationship). It is almost certainly the case that your parents did their best for you, given the limitations of their own circumstances. You have no real way of knowing what their childhoods were like. They may have told you some things about their childhoods, but they certainly won't have told you everything.

For a start, our subconscious mind tends to sanitise our more traumatic experiences from our early life, so your parents may not even know why they are the way they are. Many parents of people my age were evacuated during the war for their own safety, away from areas that were likely to be bombed. They were sent away from their natural families for years, to live in totally unfamiliar surroundings with complete strangers, often swapping a city life for a very rural one. What messages did their young minds take from that experience? On a wider level, we are never really in a position to make judgements about anybody else, certainly not without 'walking a mile in their shoes', which in the case of our parents, we can never do.

It is a mistake to look back and choose not to see their faults, just as it is unfair to be overly critical of them. They were a product of their upbringing, just as you are a product of yours. Find a balance – be realistic in your analysis of what happened and why. Learn from it, and then let it go. Forgive them their shortcomings and as a result, build a better relationship with them now. I am not suggesting that you have a conversation with them about the past – choosing to forgive is a mental exercise in your own head, and it is essentially for your benefit, not theirs.

You can do this by simply visualising conversations with them, and if you can do it under hypnosis, so much the better. There is more about this later in the book. If you do this effectively, you will feel happier in yourself and improve your relationship with them. Having done that, other relationships should then improve as well. Judith Orloff covers this subject in great detail. This process is also a great stepping stone towards forgiving yourself, which is a fundamentally important place to get to in your own personal development.

In his book *Not in your Genes*, Oliver James makes a very interesting point about the forces that govern a child's relationship with their parents.[17] He calls the phenomenon 'Offspring Stockholm Syndrome', and this is a great name for it. Stockholm Syndrome is the name given to the behaviour of hostages towards their captors. When it sinks in that a hostage is totally at the mercy of their captor, they start to try and ingratiate themselves with the captor for their own self-preservation. Their rationale is of course that the captor is less likely to kill their hostage if they like them.

What does this have to do with children? A lot, because just as the captor has the power of life or death over the hostage, so the parent has the power of life and death over their child. If the parent is a model of kindness and love, this dynamic is not particularly apparent, but if they are emotionally damaged themselves, and this is reflected in their behaviour, the similarity suddenly becomes very real. The child will inevitably feel the pressure to accept the views and behaviour of the dysfunctional parent to please or appease them, and it may ultimately become part of their own behaviour pattern, even if they started off instinctively opposed to it.

It is a very interesting analogy that explains why people can end up behaving badly towards their own children while at the same time being fully aware of how unpleasant and unacceptable being treated in that way really is.

The inner child

You will realise by now that we all have within us a younger version of ourselves that can react exactly as children do –

childishly. It will come as no surprise that the vast majority of our negative instincts are behaviours that were learned by us when we were small – in other words, they are the learned instincts of our inner child. I have already used the analogy of our different emotional ages being represented by a set of Russian dolls. So it is enormously helpful if you can picture yourself at all the crucial ages in your childhood. All those different versions of yourself are still inside you, and can still react in exactly the way that you learned to at each of those ages, even today.

Let us look at an example of how a negative self-image could have become installed in you when you were a small child. Imagine a scenario where, when you were three years old, a younger sibling arrived. Suddenly you got much less attention from your mother – she seemed to have transferred her affections from you to your new sibling. Not only does she have much less time for you, she seems less engaged with you when she does have time (because she is exhausted). You start playing up to get attention, and she just shouts at you and tells you that you are BAD. Then, horror of horrors, you are sent to kindergarten – sent away by your own mother! You could very easily jump to the conclusion that you are a bad person, and that she sent you away because of it. She clearly no longer loves you. Every single day that you are sent to kindergarten it reinforces this belief. Before long, it becomes a well-established core belief that you could carry with you for the rest of your life. It's quite depressing in some ways when you realise how easily this can happen.

Like most parents of grown-up children, I look back in horror at my lack of parenting skills when it mattered. There are so many things I wish I had done differently. Above all, I wish I had realised that if a small child is upset for no obvious reason, they need love and hugs, not an exasperated response. Most importantly, if they need telling off, make it abundantly clear that it is their behaviour, and not them, that you disapprove of.

What can you do to heal your inner child?

Looking again at the example above of the three-year-old child, what would you say to that child if you could talk to them now, and they could tell you exactly how they felt? Most people would give them a big hug, explain why the child's conclusions were completely inaccurate, and tell them they were definitely loved as much as everyone else in the family. Well the good news is it is not too late to do this, and it is very effective. It is probably even more effective under hypnosis (more on this in Chapters 8 and 9), but if you do it vividly enough, you are effectively in a state of hypnosis anyway. Done regularly, especially if you can do it every time your inner child reacts, it is extremely comforting, and extremely effective.

Seem simplistic? You are forgetting that the subconscious mind cannot tell reality from unreality; if your visualisation is powerful enough, your subconscious mind will believe that the conversation with your inner child is actually happening, and the inner child's behaviour will change as a result. If you can, get family pictures of yourself at different ages, and build strong visualisations of yourself. Spend time thinking about what your inner child was thinking and feeling at those different ages. What were their fears and worries? Have conversations with your inner child as you would if you were a loving adult that had the chance to explain the events in their life that bothered them. Visualise giving your inner child all the hugs and comfort they want.

Case study – Ron

Ron was a builder in his forties, and he came to see me because he had suffered from depression and outbursts of anger for as long as he could remember. He was single at the time he came for therapy. He described his childhood as happy, despite his father having left home when he was four. His father died soon after his fifth birthday, but he was close to his mother and he definitely felt loved by her.

Under hypnosis, we soon got to the heart of the problem. His father had left his mother for another woman, and went to live in Edinburgh. That relationship didn't work out, and he came back. He subsequently had a massive row with Ron's mother, and left again. She said that she would not have him back a second time. This happened just before Ron's fifth birthday. On his birthday, his father rang up, but the call did not go well and Ron put the phone down on him. Soon afterwards, he was told that his father had died in a car accident. Many years later, he heard that his father had actually committed suicide – he had hung himself. Subconsciously, Ron began to feel that he had caused his father to kill himself by putting the phone down on him, and consequently he began to unknowingly carry with him an immense burden of guilt.

What had actually happened was that his father had gone back up to Edinburgh to reconcile with the girlfriend he had left, and she had told him to get lost. He could not handle being alone, and hung himself in her house to punish her.

While Ron was still hypnotised, we took another look at the whole picture, and reframed it. You cannot change the past, but you can certainly change what you think about it. As we now know, changing your thoughts changes your feelings, and releases the emotional burden.

Ron could now see, at a deep level, that the phone call was totally unrelated to the chain of events that caused his father to hang himself. He had absolutely no responsibility whatever for his father's actions, and consequently no reason to feel guilty. When I brought him out of hypnosis he was extremely emotional – he said he didn't know whether to laugh or cry. He felt so unburdened that he said he felt as if he were weightless, being carried along by an invisible hot air balloon.

So how do you actually learn to love yourself?

The exercises described above can genuinely make a big difference, and I think in some cases would achieve a good level of self-love, but there is one scenario that they cannot overcome. That is where, like Ron, you are not consciously aware of the 'sensitising' event, or events, that actually caused the problem. If this is the case, you don't know what to 're-run' in your mind with your inner child - and you know my thoughts on trying to overwrite existing programs.

Much of Sigmund Freud's work studied the effect that our childhood experiences had on our adult lives, and he realised that our memories before the age of about six are particularly unreliable. They have, effectively, been reprocessed by the subconscious mind, so while they *may* be accurate, they may very well not be. You can easily verify Freud's theory for yourself. If you think back to something you did at the age of ten, you will probably recall yourself actually engaged in the action. However, if you visualise yourself doing something at the age of four, you are much more likely to see yourself from the third-party perspective - in other words, as if you were watching a film of yourself. This is because the subconscious mind has reprocessed the memory. It is particularly the traumatic events, the very ones that we are most interested in, that are the most likely to have been reprocessed. They are therefore unavailable to us for conscious reprocessing. So we need a new tool, and that tool is hypno-analysis, which is described in detail in Chapter 8.

Chapter 6

Your mind and your health

Can your conscious thoughts and subconscious programs compromise your health?

With regard to conscious thoughts, it is pretty obvious that the answer to this question is yes. Let us use stress as an example.

Worrying is the process whereby you look into the future and think about something unpleasant that might (or might not!) happen. To some extent we need to do this, firstly, so that we can take action to reduce the chances of unpleasant events occurring (a process known as mitigation), and secondly, so that we can prepare ourselves in case they do actually happen. But when you worry, you inadvertently use your powers of visualisation in a very negative way. If you regularly dwell on possible unpleasant future events (i.e. you habitually worry) long after you have done the mitigation just mentioned, this can have serious adverse effects on your health.

This is because when you think about something, you visualise it, and as previously discussed, your subconscious mind cannot tell that what you are visualising is not actually happening. So your body generates a stress response – i.e. it dumps adrenaline into your system to fire up the 'fight or flight' system when you just *think* about an unpleasant event. Adrenaline is biologically designed only to be used in short bursts, and it has serious health implications (outlined in the next section) if present in the body for extended periods. Consider also the fact that the vast majority of things which people worry about never actually happen anyway. From this perspective it soon becomes clear that at best worrying is a pointless habit, and at worst it is a potentially damaging one.

To counter this, try to get in the habit of limiting the time you spend thinking about these potentially troublesome future events, and when you have put in place all the mitigation that you can, shelve the problem. Put it in a metaphorical box, and don't keep opening it - especially at night! This is as simple as visualising yourself shutting the potential problem in a box, and putting a note on the lid regarding the date when you might choose to reopen it.

Human beings are, to some extent, victims of their own intelligence where this process is concerned. There is probably no other species that has the intelligence to look into the future and contemplate different eventualities, and without this ability they would never be able to worry, or suffer from stress-related illnesses.

Why does stress actually cause so much ill-health?

When your adrenaline levels rise, a whole raft of biochemical changes take place in your body to give you the best possible chance of escaping from the sabre-toothed tiger. These include:

1. Blood is diverted from non-essential functions (such as digestion) to the major muscle groups, such as the legs. This explains why people go white when they are frightened, because the blood supply to the skin is reduced. This in turn explains why chronically stressed people commonly get skin conditions like psoriasis and eczema, because the blood supply is insufficient to maintain healthy skin. It also explains why someone who is worried about something is described as having 'cold feet'.

2. The blood supply to your frontal cortex (the 'thinking' part of the human brain) is restricted, and deep thought becomes difficult. This is because in a highly stressful situation, you need to make snap decisions to survive. This explains why your mind can go blank during times of high stress such as exams.

3. Not only is your digestion compromised, but there is often a strong urge to 'empty the system'. If you are at risk of being eaten, digesting your lunch becomes irrelevant – better to evacuate the system and be a bit

lighter to run away! This could well be a major contributory factor to problems such as irritable bowel syndrome.

4. If you are stressed, you get more coughs and colds. Again, the immune system is very low on the priority list if the resources are needed for fighting or fleeing. If you are about to be attacked by a tiger, there is no biological advantage to wasting resources by continuing to try and fight off a cold.

5. You may have trouble sleeping – it stands to reason that if your system is on high alert you cannot at the same time relax easily and drift into a deep and restorative sleep.

6. Your breathing rate, heart rate and venous blood pressure will rise – this process is designed to get the maximum amount of oxygenated, glucose-rich blood to your muscles. Again, the system is only designed to run like this for short bursts, and the risks of permanently high blood pressure are well known.

7. It is almost inevitable in this situation that your libido will be compromised – there really is no biological advantage to having amorous feelings (let alone an erection) with a sabre-toothed tiger hot on your heels!

This is by no means an exhaustive list, but it does explain why it is so important not to accept a lifestyle that involves long-term stress. Our fight/flight system just isn't designed to operate over extended periods. The half-life of adrenaline in the body is only a few minutes, so fifteen minutes after a stressful event, the amount of adrenaline in your system should be down to a fraction of its peak level. However, if you are subjected to regular external sources of stress, or you subject yourself to internal sources by your thought patterns, you could be seriously compromising the efficiency of virtually every single one of your body's major systems on an ongoing basis. I am not sure that it is possible to rate the above list in order of importance, but continuous suppression of your immune system could not fail to have serious implications for long-term health.

The problem is that many of the triggers that cause people stress are subconsciously held beliefs, and by definition, people are completely unaware of their existence and of the potential they have to compromise their health. I have a friend with very bad psoriasis – he appears extremely laid-back, but I am absolutely sure that under analysis, a very different story would emerge.

Can you also compromise your health subconsciously?

Possibly even more damaging to your long-term health than negative thoughts, are unprocessed or 'trapped' emotions. To quote Gabor Maté again:

'Repression – dissociating emotions from awareness and relegating them to the unconscious realm – disorganises and confuses our physiological defences so that in some people these defences go awry, becoming the destroyers of health rather than its protectors.'

Anger, guilt and grief are typical emotions which some people find it difficult, or impossible, to process healthily.

It is easy to see how this happens. On many occasions I was told as a child, 'If you don't stop crying, I will really give you something to cry about'. The message here is clear – 'If you express your emotion, I will beat you'. I quickly learned that it wasn't safe to express my emotions. It took me fifty years, a fair amount of counselling and a lot of soul-searching to uninstal that program. I have read many books on this subject, and the common theme is that repressed anger and guilt are directly linked to increased rates of cancer and auto-immune diseases in later life.

As a therapist, I often see that particular chronic medical conditions are linked to specific past experiences. If the emotions generated by the past experiences are not processed effectively, they create 'trapped emotions', and specific trapped emotions appear to compromise particular organs or biological processes. This is not limited to childhood. An example of this, which I have noticed in adults is hypothyroidism, a condition where the body produces too little thyroxin. Its symptoms include tiredness, weight gain, hair loss and dry skin. I have known at least seven clients who suffer from this, and in every single case, it started when they were with bullying, overbearing partners who did not allow them to speak their mind. The thyroid is next to the larynx. Is this just a coincidence?

I am lucky enough to own a copy of Christiane Beerlandt's exhaustive work on this subject – *The Key to Self Liberation*.[18] In the book, she examines and explains the psychological origins of over 1,000 diseases and medical conditions. It is a fascinating study, and I can't tell you how many times I have looked up specific medical conditions of friends, relatives and clients and found extraordinarily close correlations between the diseases and the predicted psychological background of the person. A close friend of mine is diabetic, and the description of the mindset of a typical diabetic is so accurate it could have been written about her.

Given that there is now very strong evidence that we can inherit memory, it is no great stretch of the imagination that we could actually *inherit* attitudes from our parents, rather than *learning* them as children. If this is the case, with some diseases that are considered hereditary, maybe we are inheriting the mindset that makes us susceptible to the disease, rather than a genetic predisposition to the disease itself.

What can we learn from examining our own health history?

If we suffer from chronic medical conditions, maybe studying their psychological origins can give us another window into our subconscious mind, and specifically, the trapped emotions contained therein. Could these emotions, which have been left over from unprocessed events in our past, point us to areas we need to revisit? Maybe resolving the trapped emotion could contribute to resolving the medical condition?

Another excellent book which could help to decode the psychological messages hidden in your health history is Deb Shapiro's *Your Body Speaks Your Mind*.[19] It contains an absolute wealth of insights into the psychological roots of many medical conditions. I must emphasise that any investigation along these lines should be done in careful cooperation with your health professional – for example, never think about reducing medication without consulting your doctor.

What are psychosomatic illnesses?

Psychosomatic literally means 'mind and body', so a psychosomatic illness is a real, physical illness of the body which is partly or wholly caused by the mind. The whole theme of this book is about finding and removing the subconscious programs that can sabotage our health, happiness and relationships, and the subject of the mind/body connection involved in psychosomatic illnesses is highly relevant to my own story for two reasons: firstly, my own chain oil poisoning experience was completely psychosomatic. My mind caused me to become ill to solve what it saw as a specific problem – the fact that I was regularly inhaling a mist of mineral chain oil. Most chainsaw users do not react the way I did.

Secondly, and this is a much more common example, a very close relative of mine suffered from chronic fatigue syndrome for four years. He was totally and utterly incapacitated by it – there wasn't the slightest question that the symptoms were 100% real. He couldn't sleep, could barely concentrate to read and could only walk a few hundred metres without being totally exhausted. Working or studying was out of the question. Medical science was completely baffled and could not offer any treatment that had the slightest positive effect.

Eventually, he enrolled on a three-day training program called the *Lightning Process* which teaches attendees how to use their mind to control their biochemistry. It was created by Dr Phil Parker, and it utilises two key characteristics that we have already discussed to resolve the situation:

1. Visualisation – because the subconscious mind cannot tell reality from unreality, if you visualise the physical state that you want, rather than the one you have, regularly and clearly enough, your biochemistry changes until you create it.

2. Habituation – if you respond to a specific trigger (in this case feeling tired) in the same way every time, your subconscious mind soon takes over the therapeutic visualisation and the process becomes automated.

For my relative, the results were absolutely astounding. In less than two weeks, his problems were behind him and he never looked back. He now works long hours doing a demanding job, and there is no trace of the problem at all. I was so fascinated by the effectiveness of the *Lightning Process* that I enrolled on it myself. Its usefulness is by no means limited to resolving chronic fatigue syndrome – it is definitely another useful tool in the self-development toolbox.

This was actually the event that fired up my interest in the mind/body connection and set me on a ten-year path of study which led me to become a therapist.

If psychosomatic illnesses are to some extent created in our minds, are we to blame for them?

Therapists and medics do have to be sensitive about how they talk to clients and patients on this issue. When people hear it suggested that their illness could, to some extent, be caused by the mind, they can often display one of the following two potentially angry reactions:

1. Are you saying that I am not ill then – that I am just imagining it?
2. Are you saying it is my fault that I am ill? If I am responsible for my thoughts, then you are saying that my illness is my fault.

Both of these reactions are understandable, but they are based on a misunderstanding of how the nebulous, conceptual mind creates a real, physical illness. In law, there is a saying that 'ignorance is no plea', meaning that when accused of a crime, you cannot use as a defence the claim that you did not know you were breaking the law. The same is not true of culpability for psychosomatic illnesses. If you have a trapped emotion which you are by definition unaware of, and it is compromising your health via a mechanism that you were also unaware of, how on earth could you be considered responsible for the ensuing ill-health? It is very important that patients realise that they cannot possibly have any responsibility for something that they don't know is happening. As we have already seen, any such negative thoughts can only impede the healing process.

What can we learn from our increased understanding of the mind/body connection?

If you think about it, illnesses fall into one of three categories:

1. Those apparently caused by pathogens such as bacteria and viruses. Examples would be chickenpox or rabies.
2. Those apparently caused by environmental factors, such as asbestosis or excessive alcohol consumption.
3. Those that do not appear to have a causative agent – diabetes, lupus, hypothyroidism, rheumatism, etc.

I say 'apparently caused' for the first two categories because, even in these cases, exposure will cause some people to get ill and others not, so another factor such as the patient's mindset or emotional history is probably also involved. I am deliberately keeping cancer off the list because it is almost certainly caused by viruses (such as Human Papilloma Virus) or environmental agents (such as tobacco smoke or asbestos) in *combination* with the mindset of the patient. It would not surprise me if trapped emotions from unprocessed emotional events in the past turn out to be the *most* influential factor in determining who gets ill and who doesn't.

My point is this. Over the last few hundred years, medicine has done an outstanding job in understanding the causes and effects of illnesses in the first two categories. We have an amazing array of antibiotics and other drugs available to treat them. Medicine has made much less headway with the problems which fall into the third category.

As a layman, I would like to suggest a reason for this. Maybe it is because modern medicine has followed a 'reductionist' path when studying illnesses until, as the saying goes, it has 'failed to see the wood for the trees'. Microscopes have got more and more powerful, until we can see the tiniest cells, bacteria, viruses and even molecules. The problem is that however powerful your microscope, you will never spot a human mind under it! Looking at disease in the body without considering the potential input from the mind is known as 'dualism'. Fortunately, non-dualism is gaining ground, and even scientists who have linked specific illnesses to particular genes are forced to admit that other factors, including mental attitude, have a significant effect on whether or not illness actually develops.

It is not even much of a mystery that your mind can have such a powerful effect on your health. Clearly our thoughts can affect our hormone levels – sexual arousal is a good example – and hormone levels have been directly linked to specific diseases, for example cancer of the reproductive system. It seems logical to me that any illness that can be improved or alleviated in some way by the mind could have been partially or completely caused by the mind in the first place. For me, the effectiveness of the Lightning Process, and the very existence of the placebo effect, provide strong evidence for this. Add to this the observed correlation between specific illnesses and particular psychological experiences and it's hard not to conclude that modern medicine is not looking in the right place in its attempt to resolve 'Category 3' illnesses.

To some people, nothing I am saying here is news. To them, the connection between our mental health and our physical health is crystal clear. Louise Hay's seminal work in this field was published forty years ago. Her book, *Heal Your Body* has been through over ninety editions and reprints.[20] What totally baffles me is why this has still not yet become a mainstream idea – the vast majority of people remain totally unaware of what is, to the minority, blindingly obvious. The old adage 'healthy body, healthy mind' originally meant that to be mentally healthy we should take exercise and stay physically fit. In other words, if you are feeling down, go out for a walk. But the opposite is even more true – if you want a healthy body, you must work to achieve a truly healthy mind. Recent research by Dr Bruce Lipton, Dr Candace Pert and others has simply exposed the mechanisms that make this happen.

The link between illness and trapped emotion is actually an example of what is known as the 'nocebo effect', which is where, instead of a positive thought making you well, a negative thought or emotion makes you ill. To quote Dr Bruce Lipton:

'While proper use of consciousness can bring health to an ailing body, inappropriate unconscious control of emotions can make a healthy body diseased.'

Interestingly, research has shown that placebo pills have more effect if their shape, colour and size are, in the patient's opinion, suited to the illness.[21] For example, blue is apparently considered the optimal colour for sedatives, and red for heart pills. Also, if drug companies suddenly change the colour of a pill, there is a marked increase in people stopping their medication, presumably because they no longer have confidence that it will work.

To drug companies, the placebo effect is an annoyance that massively increases the costs of testing the efficacy of new drugs.

If they spent half as much time and money working out how to reliably trigger the placebo effect, rather than how to remove its effects from their statistics, the world would be a happier and healthier place. But this would of course mean that we wouldn't need most of the drugs which they produce, so don't hold your breath while you wait for it to happen!

It is easy to get the impression that over the years, science in general has been slow to investigate phenomena which do not fit nicely into the Newtonian Theory of Physics or the Darwinian Theory of Evolution. It has been easier to conveniently ignore evidence that doesn't fit in with mainstream scientific beliefs than to try and explain *why* it doesn't fit in. But in more recent times, increasing knowledge in previously unheard of fields such as quantum mechanics and epigenetics has moved phenomena such as faith healing and Extrasensory Perception (ESP) from the inexplicable to the potentially explicable. It's hard not to get the impression that medicine has been slower than other disciplines to make that mental shift, and the immense wealth and power of the drug companies is almost certainly a factor in this.

If you can't see the wood for the trees, what happens?

The net result of continuing with the dualist approach, this lack of ability to see the bigger picture, is that modern medicine spends much of its time treating the symptom, not the problem. If you go to the doctor with psoriasis, he is much more likely to give you some hydrocortisone cream to rub on than to ask you what is causing you to feel stressed. As an aside, one of the things that puzzles me about stress-related illnesses is that, generally speaking, people often only get one. My friend who is so troubled with psoriasis, has no obvious problems with his digestive or immune systems, and he sleeps like a log. I know other people who really suffer with irritable bowel syndrome, but their skin is fine.

There are several other related problems at play in our modern health service. The first is that as we learn more about how the human body works, doctors are forced to become more specialised, and the more specialised they are, the harder it is for them to see the bigger picture. The second problem is that as medical resources become ever more stretched, time is at a premium. Specialists have less time with each patient to really find out the key background information that might point them towards the cause of a condition, rather than just its symptoms. Thirdly, as increasingly sophisticated diagnostic equipment has become available, a wealth of medical instinct and intuition from a wide range of cultures has been lost.

Until medicine in general sees what is happening, it will be down to the individual to find therapists who can help them to identify the real issues that lie behind their medical symptoms. This is exactly how I eventually resolved my chain oil problem.

There is a school of thought that considers that physical symptoms are gifts that offer us the opportunity to heal ourselves at a much deeper level. The inability to work eventually enabled me to realise that I was inadvertently poisoning myself, and to stop doing it. I am not suggesting for one minute that if you are getting blinding headaches that you should be delighted, or that you should go to a hypnotist rather than getting a brain scan. But if you have a long-term illness such as an auto-immune disease that medical science is failing to resolve, I am certainly suggesting that there are other options available.

Are individual emotions linked to specific organs in the body?

This concept has been accepted since the time of the Greeks, and probably before that, and it is still reflected in the language we use today. The liver has always been associated with anger for example, and when people are really angry we say that they are livid. The heart, of course, is associated with joy and love, so when people are free with these emotions we refer to them as open-hearted. Conversely, when they are unfeeling, we refer to them as being hard-hearted, or cold-hearted. The kidneys are associated with fear, and possibly this is not unrelated to the fact that people potentially wet themselves when they are very frightened.

This concept linking emotions to specific organs gradually fell out of favour when medicine became reductionist, and effectively changed from being an art based largely on instincts to a science based largely on observable evidence. When these organs were examined under a microscope, no evidence was found that such ideas had any physical basis. However, now that many of the cells in these organs are found to be covered in receptors for the neurotransmitters that communicate these emotions, the concept is beginning to make a lot more sense again.

But if this is true, how does the knowledge help us?

Let us suppose we have been badly hurt by the breakup of a relationship, and it leaves us feeling emotionally numb for a while. This is pure speculation, but maybe there is actually a biochemical process that is designed to protect our heart from further pain. Given the extraordinary sophistication of the mind/body connections that scientists are currently uncovering, this is not so far-fetched. And if this is the case, why would we not actively visualise dismantling this barrier when we are ready to enter another relationship? Visualising implies seeing something, and although we can't actually see emotions, we can visualise a barrier that covers our heart dissolving away so that the emotions of love and joy can be given and received. You can obviously add to this visualisation by imagining the emotion as a coloured light that is then able to shine both ways. When I had this idea, I tried it under hypnosis, and really felt profoundly different afterwards. It is now part of my regular practice.

What actually happens when we visualise things?

I mention visualisation quite a lot in the next few chapters because it is an extremely powerful tool which is very easy to use. Generally speaking, in our normal conscious state, visualisation temporarily reprograms the subconscious mind, but under hypnosis, its effects are much more powerful. To understand why our subconscious is so easily fooled by images that we plant in it consciously, consider this question:

Can we see things that we cannot imagine, or that we do not believe exist?

This might sound like a strange question, but there is a reason for asking it. When you look at an object, your eye does not form a picture of it and send the picture to your brain. We know this in two ways:

1. Nerves send electrical impulses (i.e. data, not pictures), and it is only when that data is interpreted in the visual

cortex of the brain that its meaning (i.e. the picture) is revealed.

2. Very occasionally, there have been people who have been blind from birth who have had operations as adults to enable them to see. When they wake up from the operation they do not see their surroundings when they open their eyes. Apparently, it takes weeks for their brains to learn to interpret the information and create usable vision.

This concept is also supported by stories from Captain Cook's voyages to remote islands in the Southern Pacific. It is reported that when he anchored the Endeavour in a bay and rowed ashore in a smaller boat, the natives could see the small boat, but not the large one with the masts and rigging. The suggestion is that they could see the small boat because it was sufficiently similar to their own dugouts, but the large vessel was so far beyond their comprehension that they could literally not imagine it. The word 'imagine' means 'to form an image of', so the idea is that their brains were literally unable to form the image of what their eyes were trying to communicate.

This does make some sense, and it might explain a few other phenomena. The Captain Cook story is totally analogous to the situation with UFOs today. Plenty of people claim to have seen them, and if I have not, is it simply because I just don't believe they exist?

Almost the world over, children's stories involve 'little people' – elves, fairies, trolls, pixies, leprechauns and so on. They are a common theme in stories from every corner of the world and children quite often say that they have seen them – they have their little friend at the end of the garden. I have had several clients who swore this was so. Is it possible that the 'little people' do actually exist, but that as we grow up, we cease to be able to see them simply because we are told by adults that they do not exist? Once we become convinced of this, because children are highly suggestible, we cease to be able to see what we no longer believe to be there.

The same thing is true of people's auras – many children claim to be able to see coloured auras around people (without having ever heard of them), but very few adults can see them. Having said that, the adults that can see them are absolutely adamant that they exist. Maybe this phenomenon would also explain those slightly puzzling car accidents when otherwise good drivers pull out of a junction in front of an oncoming vehicle. Possibly as they approached the junction they for some reason 'believed' that the road would be clear, and then failed to see the vehicle which they did not believe existed?

There is of course a potential flaw in this argument – when we are born we would theoretically have no knowledge of what anything looked like, so we wouldn't be able to see anything at all! I am of course aware that newborn babies see very little – I am referring to the time when their sight becomes fully developed. My answer would be that before the age of about three, we are very highly suggestible, and accept information presented to us without question. It is only as we get older that we develop the ability to judge whether information is correct, true or valid. Also, since it has been demonstrated that we can inherit memory, maybe we inherit the belief that most of the things around us exist.

This idea has real relevance to visualisation. If, as I suggest, the image we see is created in the brain by messages from the eye, how does the image actually differ from one presented to the brain by messages from the conscious mind in the form of a visualisation? Possibly not at all, which would explain why visualisation can so easily dupe the subconscious mind into believing that the image it is being presented with is real.

Incidentally, the word 'visualise' is slightly misleading in the sense that we are using it – it sounds as if it only applies to pictures, but in truth we can 'visualise' input from any of the five senses. We can, for instance 'visualise' the feel of fur or sandpaper, or the smell of cut grass or wood smoke. The word 'imagine' isn't any less visual, and I don't often use it because for me it definitely carries a stronger implication that the thing you are imagining is not actually there. This is, of course, exactly the opposite of the idea we are trying to create.

Further reading - a compelling example of healing using the mind/body connection

In his amazing book, *Secrets of Aboriginal Healing*, Gary Holz describes his journey from being a wheelchair-bound, terminally ill multiple sclerosis sufferer to throwing away his wheelchair and travelling the world, lecturing on his amazing recovery in the hands of a tribe of aborigines deep in the Australian outback.[22]

Until the arrival of the white man, aborigines had no access at all to modern diagnostic equipment, and they learned a system of healing which involves understanding the mind/body connection in great depth. In this specific respect, it cannot be denied that aborigines really are far ahead of western medicine. From reading Gary Holz's book, it is clear that they associate specific ailments with particular psychological experiences, and use kinesiology and talking therapies to achieve resolution of some illnesses which western doctors are still completely puzzled by.

Even further reading

In his book *It's the Thought that Counts*, Dr David Hamilton thoroughly reviews decades of research that provides a wealth of evidence for the mind/body connection and the undoubted influence that our thoughts have over our health. To quote him directly:

'*It is now known that there is an entire psychosomatic network connecting the body and mind, involving hundreds of neuropeptides and thousands of receptor locations throughout the body. Any of a vast range of thoughts or feelings can cause a whole cascade of changes in a person's body.*'[23]

He covers the demonstrable benefits of meditation and also reviews scientific studies of distant healing which demonstrate conclusively that patients who are regularly prayed for have better medical outcomes that those who are not. The concept of the 'collective unconscious' is also discussed, likening a group of human minds to a network of computers. Although he doesn't mention it, I have always thought that the existence of the collective consciousness is beautifully demonstrated by the simultaneous turns and movements of flocks of birds and shoals of fish. I can see no other explanation of how this is possible.

Above all, Dr Hamilton's message is that our attitudes and our intentions are fundamental, not only to our own health and happiness, but also to those of the people around us, and in a wider sense, to humanity as a whole.

Another groundbreaking book on the subject of the mind/body connection is Patricia Worby's *The Scar that Won't Heal*.[24] It explains how our early human survival strategies are maladapted to our 21st century lives which are full of chronic, and often subconscious, stress. She explains how any experience, if it occurs in a state of helplessness, can be considered traumatic. These would include a difficult birth, separation, accident, bereavement, surgery, poor parenting, bullying, abuse, etc. It is immediately obvious that very few people escape a childhood without at least some of these experiences, and this supports my contention that there is hardly a person alive who would not benefit in some way from some form of therapy.

Many books have been written on this subject from either a scientific or clinical point of view, and they usually focus either on psychology or physiology, but Patricia Worby's book does both. Like this book, it aims to explain to an intelligent lay reader the processes involved in a way that unifies theory and practice towards a new understanding of chronic illness. It is written for those with chronic fatigue syndrome, fibromyalgia and other forms of chronic disease, or for those who love and care for them, so that they may gain understanding of how they got to be the way they are – and, more importantly, how they can recover.

Chapter 7

Time for some solutions

If I were reading this book, I would by now be more than ready for some concrete suggestions as to how to make serious progress in achieving the level of personal development which has been described. As the author, I hope that from my unvarnished description of my past, it is abundantly clear that I have made some big steps towards emotional maturity. I don't think anyone ever achieves this completely, but I feel that I am light-years ahead of where I was, even five years ago. I can now see that as a young man, I was an irritable, stressed, needy, adrenaline junkie who was utterly hopeless at personal relationships – and those were just my good points!

Things are very different now. I'm much more grounded, genuinely calm and am far better at friendships in general - and relationships in particular. How did I get there? If I had to put a toolkit together to achieve this now, it would include the following:

1. Creative visualisation
2. Reframing
3. Kinesiology
4. Mindful habituation

5. Inner Child work

6. Reverse engineering one's biochemistry

7. Taking advantage of the natural hypnosis that occurs either side of sleep

8. Breathing to reduce stress

9. Learning forgiveness

10. Creating a hypnotic script based around one's own health

11. Studying one's dreams

12. Being hypno-analysed

13. Learning and using self-hypnosis

The first eleven suggestions can be easily learned, and utilised on a daily basis. The last two are more complicated and profound, and I describe them in detail in the next two chapters. There is no 'one size fits all' solution. Some people find that certain things work better than others. I tried some therapies that just didn't work at all for me, but the ones listed here all had very positive outcomes. Let's look at each of them in turn.

1. The power of creative visualisation

Visualisation is a very, very useful tool, and is really easy to use. It relies on the simple fact that your subconscious mind is completely unable to distinguish reality from unreality. If you don't believe this, sit quietly in a chair for a few minutes and visualise lying on a tropical beach in the shade of a palm tree. Hear the sound of the surf, and the seabirds calling, feel the sand beneath your body - really visualise it clearly. Most people who do this will soon find that they feel calmer, and their pulse rate and blood pressure are measurably lower. Consciously, you knew you were in your living room, but subconsciously, your body reacted as if you were on the beach. The same is true watching a film. Consciously, you know you are in the cinema, but your subconscious still dumps adrenaline into your bloodstream when something alarming happens.

So how can you use this knowledge to really improve your life? If you visualise something which you want to happen in the future (it needs to be something that you have some control over, like the outcome of an interview, or passing a driving test), then your subconscious will be fooled into thinking it is definitely going to happen. Your subconscious will then optimise your behaviour in line with achieving that outcome. The intended outcome obviously needs to be achievable – do not visualise being able to fly and then jump off the roof of your house!

Top sportsmen and sportswomen do this all the time. Watch any athlete before an event. They spend quiet time 'getting into the zone'. What they are actually doing is shutting out the distractions around them and giving 100% of their attention to a clear visualisation of themselves producing their best possible performance. As they then compete, they trust their subconscious mind to help them deliver the performance they visualised. This technique is incredibly useful for short-term fixes – it does not permanently re-program your subconscious in life-changing ways like hypnotherapy does, but it can massively improve your ability to achieve your short-term goals on a day-to-day basis. If you are giving up alcohol, visualising yourself having a lime and soda will make it much more likely to happen a few hours later down the pub. For a much more in-depth look at this subject, read *Creative Visualization* by Shakti Gawain.[25]

2. The power of reframing – choosing your thoughts, and consequently your emotions

Most people think that they have little or no control over their emotions, but this is far from true. The majority of your emotions are directly generated by your thoughts, and while you can't always choose what happens to you, you can clearly choose what you think about it. The obvious implication of this is that if you deliberately change the thought, the new thought will trigger a different emotion, so you *do* have control over your emotions. This process is known as reframing.

Here is an excellent practical example. You are driving along, and an idiot overtakes you dangerously and cuts in front of you. He then carries on his lunatic driving style and continues on his adrenaline-fuelled journey. You might well conclude that he was selfish and was unnecessarily endangering you and other drivers for the hell of it, and this could well make you angry and stressed (which does *you* no good at all, and also does *him* no harm at all!) An alternative scenario might be that he has a very sick child in the car and he is desperate to get the child to hospital. If you chose this interpretation instead, you would not be remotely stressed by his driving style, and you would wish him well. End result? You feel better. You will never know the truth of what motivated him to drive dangerously, but your active choice to reinterpret the facts clearly benefits you. No one else is affected in any way. Why would you not choose to do this as a matter of course? Get in the habit of looking for interpretations that generate calming emotions instead of stress-inducing ones.

Very often in life, when things go wrong, they actually work out for the best in the end. With the value of hindsight, we can see that most clouds do have silver linings. So when things go wrong, rather than feeling sad or unhappy, why not remain optimistic, believing that there will be an upside and waiting to see what it is? Whether you see a glass as half full or half empty is absolutely your choice, and the choice you make (your thought) determines how you subsequently feel (your emotion). It is within the power of all of us to do this on an ongoing basis.

While on the subject of happiness, here is a saying by Rabbi Hyman Schachtel that is worth thinking about:

Happiness is not having what you want, but wanting what you have. [26]

In other words, a conscious change in our own attitude can make the difference as to whether we are happy or not. It is within the power of all of us to make that decision. If you simply make the choice to think that you are lucky with your lot in life, your new thought generates a new emotion – happiness. 'Having what you want' essentially implies that you have enough money to buy what you want – and this is why some people think that having money will make them happy. But it isn't actually having the object that pleases people, it is the experience of acquiring the object. This is why some people regard shopping as a leisure activity, but unless you keep doing it, constantly buying bigger and better stuff, it ceases to work. I know for a fact that having 'stuff' doesn't make me happy. When I got divorced, I went from a three-bedroom house to one rented room at a friend's house. I got rid of everything that did not fit in that one room, and I found the experience very cathartic - I have never been acquisitive since. Money doesn't make people happy - the best thing you can say about it is that it allows you to be miserable in comfort!

If you stand back and take an honest look at your life in the context of how most people in the world live, it is blindingly obvious that those of us in developed countries should all be grateful for what we have. Unless you are seriously ill, you are probably in the top 10%, if not much higher, in terms of health, wealth, comfort and safety. If you cultivate a genuine sense of gratitude, it would be illogical not to be fundamentally happy. This is the ultimate act of reframing.

3. Kinesiology, and how it can help you

Kinesiology, or muscle testing, allows the therapist to let the client's body give answers to questions that they are unable to respond to consciously. As discussed, if you were the client, you would be asked to hold your arm out horizontally, and the therapist would ask you to make a statement. If the statement was in conflict with your subconscious belief, your muscle strength would be noticeably weaker, and the therapist could sense this by applying slight downward pressure on your arm. It can also be used to determine whether or not you are allergic to certain chemicals, plants, etc, as evidenced by my chain oil poisoning.

Conventional medicine finds it hard to explain how this phenomenon works, but there is absolutely no doubt among therapists of the validity of this methodology. As previously described, there are a growing number of people who believe that your mind is not in your head, but in the whole of your body. This may sound like a bizarre idea, but there is evidence to support it.

Psychological kinesiology, where the client makes statements (such as 'I deserve to be treated with love and respect'), can be enormously useful to the therapist. Few people would consciously disagree with this statement, but if their arm goes weak when being muscle-tested, it suggests that their subconscious programming is not supporting it. This might explain, for example, why some people continually make poor relationship choices. Events in their past have programmed their subconscious into this unhealthy belief, and they are unknowingly trapped in a cycle of bad relationships as a result. Fortunately, hypno-analysis enables the programming to be permanently changed.

Somewhat bizarrely, there are some experienced kinesiologists who can perform muscle testing on a client without actually asking them to make the statements. They just think the statement, and 'interrogate' the client's body. If I had not experienced this, I would have been highly dubious of such a claim, but I have seen it work. Most kinesiologists put their free hand on the client's shoulder, to complete a kind of energy loop. They also ask the client to keep their head level, but look down, as if they were looking at their own cheeks. The reason for this is that the direction in which your eyes look is indicative of the part of the brain that you are accessing. If you don't believe this, imagine asking someone to recall a distant memory – they will almost always look up as they try and remember. This can also be a sign of lying, because it accesses the imagination in a similar way. So kinesiologists want you to look down so that they get an honest response, unaffected by what you imagine or wish the answer to be.

There are various ways that you can learn to muscle-test yourself. Here are three suggestions:

a) Using your thumbs and first fingers, make two circles and interlock them. With the correct amount of thumb to fingertip pressure, you can then try and pull the circles apart. Make a statement, then see if you can separate them – with a positive response they fail to separate, but a negative response allows them to pull apart.

b) Place your left hand on a table with your index finger raised. Place your other hand at right angles to it so that the pad of your little finger rests on the nail of the left index finger. Flex the left index finger, then use the right little finger to push down on it as you make your statements. This simulates, on a small scale, someone else using their hand to push down your arm.

c) Stand a few inches away from a wall, facing away from it. Set your feet a comfortable distance apart, relax and close your eyes. Be aware of your balance, spreading your weight over the whole area of your feet. Make the statement you wish to test. You will either tend to sway forwards, which is a positive result, or backwards, which is a negative result. The wall is there to stop you falling over backwards if you get a strong negative reaction!

It is important that during this process you keep your mind on the statement and do not say it mindlessly while your thoughts are elsewhere.

4. Mindful habituation

Don't bother searching for this phrase – I made it up. What I mean by it is being sufficiently self-aware to notice when your subconsciously-driven behaviour is not as you would like it to be, and make a really conscious effort to change it. This would include the way you relate to other people, as well as your pastimes and daydreams – everything about you. To make effective changes, you need to identify and correct the undesirable behaviour *every single time* that it occurs. This is what I did with my catastrophic daydreams, and because of our instinctive urge to form habits, it eventually happens automatically. I rarely have those daydreams now, but I still jump on them when they occur. The key to this is to be as mindful as possible – to notice your thoughts and actions and analyse them. They may be normal to you, but are they really 'normal' in the wider sense? When I look back at my disaster-strewn life, it's clear that my thoughts and actions were not normal by most people's standards.

5. Inner child work

I have already described this in some detail. It is not hard to do, although it can be very emotional, and it can make a profound difference to the way that we feel about ourselves. It is a therapeutic process that truly heals a part of us inside that is hurting. The vast majority of occasions when we are not proud of what we have said or done were the result of acting without emotional maturity. If we heal the inner child, it pays off in several ways – we are happier, we like ourselves more and we get on better with other people. When the inner child is healed, our actions and reactions are consistently grown-up, and we can claim to have gained some level of emotional maturity. At that point, we hold the key, not just to having amazing personal relationships, but to keeping them amazing because our interpersonal behaviour never deteriorates. We are, in a sense, becoming more closely the person we would have been if we had been born into a perfect world where we never picked up any negative programs in the first place.

6. Reverse engineering your biochemistry

Most people are aware that there is a close correlation between their mood and their posture. If you feel happy and confident, you stand tall and make expansive gestures. If you are sad and/or nervous, you shrink and sit all hunched up. What far fewer people realise is that by consciously changing your posture, you can reverse engineer your body chemistry (i.e. how you feel) to achieve the outcome you want, rather than the one you currently have. It has been demonstrated time and again with blood tests that changes to more expansive postures lower levels of stress hormones and raise levels of hormones associated with happiness and confidence. Once you have flooded your body with the hormones you want, your more positive biochemistry improves your attitude and your body language. This is an especially useful tool before potentially stressful meetings and interviews. It's just another example of 'fake it till you make it'.

7. Using natural hypnotism

As we slip between being awake and being asleep, we transition through a hypnotic state. The same thing occurs as we wake up. The state is easily recognisable once you know what you are looking for. For me, it is characterised by two things. Firstly, my limbs feel so heavy that it seems quite difficult to move them. Secondly, I see moving patterns under my eyelids. In this state, your suggestibility is heightened considerably, and it is much easier to instal thoughts and ideas at a deeper level than normal. This is a very good reason to keep your thoughts positive before going to bed, because negative thoughts and ideas can very easily be installed inadvertently. Get into the habit of using this time to indulge in some positive self-talk, and visualise yourself achieving your dreams.

8. Breathing to reduce stress

Have you ever noticed that your heart rate goes up when you breathe in, and down when you breathe out? The reason for this is that breathing in stimulates your sympathetic nervous system, which is responsible for your state of arousal (your fight or flight response), and breathing out stimulates your parasympathetic nervous system, which is responsible for your body's activities at rest. A sudden shock is associated with a sharp intake of breath for a reason. If you sit down in your favourite chair to relax, you are likely to do so with a long 'sighing out' breath. Therefore, if you consciously inhale a deep breath reasonably quickly, but let it out reasonably slowly, it cannot fail to calm you down. If you keep doing this while you are relaxing, it makes a significant contribution to lowering your stress level.

9. Learn forgiveness

I have always suspected that holding grudges was probably not a healthy thing to do, so when I was younger I used to live by a simple rule: *never hold a grudge for more than 25 years!* With the greater insight that I now possess about how negative emotions can affect us, I have reduced the time limit to 25 seconds. This is plenty of time to realise that the only person who will be affected by carrying resentment is you. I am not suggesting that people should not be held accountable for their behaviour, but being unforgiving only causes further pain to the injured party. I do acknowledge that this is sometimes more easily said than done, but it is very cathartic when you can manage it. I remember many years ago, hearing a man whose daughter had been murdered by the IRA at Enniskillen saying that he forgave the perpetrators. His name was Gordon Wilson, and it was humbling to listen to him. He went on to become an active peace campaigner. At the time, I could not even imagine ever being able to find that kind of forgiveness in me – and I hope I never have to.

It is one of the tragedies of the human condition that emotional damage and the ensuing bad behaviour is frequently handed down from one generation to the next. Sadly, the innocent children of drug addicts, alcoholics and abusers are far more likely to end up living similarly dysfunctional lives than those of us who, by chance, were brought up in happier circumstances. Everyone's bad behaviour has a cause at some level which we are frequently not in a position to know. If we fail to forgive them, we are said to bear resentment, or to hold, or carry, a grudge. Think about this for a minute – anything which you bear, hold or carry is a burden to you. Why would you choose to carry a burden that has no benefit to you, and does not adversely affect the person who wronged you in any way at all? It simply makes no sense.

Could I ask you to stop reading for a while and think of someone towards whom you bear some resentment? Then imagine how it would feel if you could just let that resentment go – visualise as clearly as you can, telling them that you forgive them and that you are letting go of any bad feeling towards them. When I have done this myself, it has felt absolutely liberating. The reality is that, to achieve this, you don't have to communicate with the person at all – it is just a mental exercise. If you want to make it more real, write to them – you don't have to send the letter. If you want to go even further, you can write a reply in response to yours, putting yourself in their position. If you do this, it is more effective if the letters are handwritten than typed. If it sounds a bit mad, all I can say is don't knock it until you have tried it. It is, in reality, a specialised form of reframing.

Now that you have hopefully felt the benefit of this, try and work out who in your life you find it hardest to forgive for their mistakes. If you are honest and self-aware, the chances are that you will realise that it is YOU. Many people seem predisposed to set themselves higher standards than they expect others to meet, and give themselves a harder time when they fail to meet those standards. If you do this consistently, you end up continuously weighed down by an invisible burden. We ALL periodically get things wrong and fail to achieve what is expected of us. If we benefit when we forgive others in these situations, we benefit even more when we learn to forgive ourselves, and it is not hard to do. You simply need to find some quiet time, and view what you did from a third-party perspective. Ask some questions: why did you do it, what were the extenuating circumstances, what did you learn from the experience, will you do it again? If, with this new perspective, it is something that you could forgive someone else for, then why on earth would you not forgive yourself? Have that conversation in your mind. Remember, as I have said so many times before - if you visualise something clearly enough, your subconscious mind will think it is actually happening. You can do this going right back through your life, having as many conversations with your inner child as you need to. Doing it under hypnosis is even more effective.

10. Write a bespoke hypnotic script that addresses the underlying causes of your own ill-health

When I read Louise Hay's book *Heal Your Body*, I had an idea that might just go a long way to addressing the underlying psychological issues that from time to time manifested themselves in my body as disease. I decided to make a note of any and every medical condition I had ever suffered from – laryngitis, nose bleeds, a slipped disc, etc. – and make a note of the positive affirmations that she suggests in her book to resolve them. By the time I did this, I was a qualified hypnotist, so I wrote them into a hypnotic script which was modelled on the delightful closing meditation which she includes at the end of her book. This meditation in itself is intended to create a healthy consciousness and a healthy mind, and I now have my own customised version of it.

I sent the script to another hypnotist I know whose style and voice I particularly liked, and she sent a recording of it back to me as an MP3. Because I am able to hypnotise myself, I now put myself into trance and play the recording regularly. If you can't hypnotise yourself, this is not a problem – you simply ask the therapist to include a hypnotic induction and deepener before the script. For those unfamiliar with the process of hypnosis, inductions and deepeners form the preamble that a therapist uses to relax the client before addressing the issue in question.

11. Study your dreams and ask them what you need to know

Use the power of your subconscious - and seek the wisdom of your intuition - by studying your dreams. We learned in Chapter 1 that our subconscious mind is many, many times more powerful than our conscious mind, so it makes perfect sense to access that power. In Chapter 4, we learned much more about the accessibility and significance of our dreams. We all have intuition, and while we may consciously struggle to tune in to it, our dreams give us instant access to it. Intuition is undoubtedly a subconscious function, so dreams offer an easy way to access it and it makes no sense not to use it.

Chapter 8

Hypno-analysis - the cream of therapies

Let me say something to start. I do not describe hypno-analysis as the cream of therapies because I am a hypno-analyst. The boot is firmly on the other foot. I became a hypno-analyst because I experienced at first hand the extraordinarily profound beneficial effects of the therapy. Once you appreciate the power of the subconscious mind, and the significance of the programs it is running, you also appreciate that you need a tool that gives you access to the subconscious mind, and a technique to search out and change the programs. Hypnosis is the tool, and analysis is the technique.

What is hypnosis?

Before explaining hypno-analysis, I need to explain what the hypnotic state is. Hypnosis is defined as a state of deep relaxation enabling Effortless Selective Thinking. What this means is that the client becomes so relaxed that they naturally lose awareness of their surroundings and concentrate 100% on a specific subject – in this case the concepts the therapist is talking about. It is actually a completely natural state which most people achieve for themselves on a very regular basis. If you daydream, you have hypnotised yourself. If you are engrossed in a film or a book, you are in a state of hypnosis. If you drive somewhere, and don't remember parts of the journey, you were hypnotised. Every time you go to sleep or wake up, you transition through a hypnotic state. It is completely safe and natural.

It is because the client usually hears every word that the therapist says that clients often claim that 'it didn't work'. However, there are clear signs that clients are in hypnosis, so the therapist is much better placed to make that judgement. Clients will hear what the therapist says whether they are hypnotised or not. Hypnotised people are generally unaware of their surroundings, so they appear to the uninitiated to be asleep, but they are actually in a heightened state of awareness. It is because people confuse hypnosis with a sleep-like state that they think that hearing the therapist signifies that they weren't hypnotised.

It is possible, although it is not common in my experience, for a client to transition from hypnosis to sleep during a therapy session. However, it is only the conscious mind that sleeps – the subconscious is still awake and still listening - and the therapy still works.

The significance of the hypnotic state is that the Conscious Critical Faculty (CCF – referred to in Chapter 1) is suspended, and this has two hugely important implications. Firstly, it allows new programs to be installed in the subconscious, such as 'I deserve to be treated with love and respect', or 'I only eat and drink what my body truly needs'. Secondly, it allows access to memories and emotions that have been deeply buried – once expressed they can be released, and they lose their toxic effect on us.

Given that it is pretty much impossible to get to adulthood without picking up a few (or many!) unhelpful core beliefs and repressed emotions, there are very few people who would not benefit from hypno-analysis, and quite a few whose lives could be absolutely transformed by it.

What is hypno-analysis?

Hypno-analysis is a process of psychoanalysis, conducted while the client is hypnotised. It is fundamentally a simple and relaxing process where the therapist guides the client back in time under hypnosis (usually to their childhood), allowing them to revisit events which continue to adversely affect their adult life. These events are not always traumatic, but for one reason or another, they continue to trigger unwanted thoughts or behaviours. During analysis, the client is able to re-experience the event, but also to view it from an adult perspective. This can be an extremely cathartic experience, and allows the event to be completely detoxified from an emotional point of view.

On a practical level, having hypnotised the client, the therapist invites them to let their mind drift back to their childhood, and describe whatever comes into their head. As this 'free association' occurs, the subconscious mind is drawn to the events which have unresolved emotional content, and they become much more real to the client than if they just remembered the event in a normal waking state. It is the re-experiencing of the emotions felt at the time that allows them to be discharged, and consequently the emotions then lose their ability to affect the behaviour of the adult.

The process is usually undertaken in hourly sessions at weekly intervals, and after 6-12 weeks, the client usually feels a sense of lightness - as if they have been relieved of a burden they did not know they were carrying. If the process was thorough, the effects will be permanent. Considered to be far quicker and more effective than conscious psychoanalysis, it is regarded by many exponents as a truly exceptional therapy.

There are two different ways of approaching it, depending on the problem that the client is presenting with:

1. Direct Regression to Cause (DRC) is 'therapist-led' and follows a specific path. In other words, the therapist seeks to engage the client in a recent memory of the subject in question, and then encourages them to search

for and re-experience successively older but directly related memories, until they encounter and re-experience the original event which caused the current symptom pattern. The client is therefore being guided along a chronological chain of Secondary Sensitising Events (SSEs) until he/she encounters the Initial Sensitising Event (ISE). At this point, a thorough emotional release (abreaction) would hopefully 'detoxify' the event, and a successful resolution would be expected. By definition, this is therefore seen as a 'single issue' therapy. It is ideal for problems such as phobias. Important note – describing a process as 'therapist-led' means that the therapist leads the direction that the therapy follows. It does not imply that the therapist leads what the client says. For instance, the therapist might ask, 'When is the first time you remember feeling like that?' This is not the same as leading the client in a way that could potentially generate false memories – a situation which all therapists should be trained to avoid.

2. Free association is a Freudian model of therapy which is much more 'client led', with only minimal input from the therapist. It is a process where a client in therapy allows their mind to wander through their memories without any conscious 'steering' from the therapist. Under hypnosis, once the client's conscious control of their

train of thought is released, their subconscious mind takes over and memories will come to them for no apparent reason. Neither their significance, nor their connection to each other, will be apparent – and they shouldn't even try to work it out – they just let the memories keep coming. And this becomes easy, because in this deeply relaxed state, the Conscious Critical Faculty is suspended and their recall is enhanced, so their memories will flow effortlessly, one after another.

The flow of this stream of thoughts is not really a random process. The memories are actually being selected by the client's subconscious mind because they have connections with the events which are causing problems in their daily life. As they describe these events, they will also feel and describe the emotions they felt at the time they occurred. To start with, they will just be circling around the issues, but before long, events and emotions will surface that will allow real healing to take place. The client just needs to go with the flow and allow their subconscious mind to work effortlessly on their behalf.

The events will not be chronologically ordered, and are linked by their emotional content, which will not be obvious to the client and probably not to the therapist either. In subsequent sessions, the memories would be expected to have increasing emotional content until abreaction occurs. More than one abreaction would be likely, although intensity would vary depending on the emotional content of the memory and the personality type of the client. Warriors tend to display the least emotion, and Nomads the most.

I do not regard one method as being more or less valid than the other *per se*, because I think they simply have different applications. If, after a thorough initial consultation, it appears to the therapist that a single issue underlies the symptoms the client is presenting, Direct Regression to Cause would probably be suitable. However, if the consultation exposed a childhood which was troubled on several levels, the 'free association' approach would seem much more appropriate.

If you wonder whether talking with the therapist will bring you out of hypnosis, the opposite is actually true. As the client talks about their past, they become more involved in the recollection, and can frequently slip into a deeper trance as a result. With either therapy, it is really important that the client tells the therapist everything that comes to mind, even if it seems really trivial, or even if they might consider it embarrassing. In fact, memories with strong emotional content of any sort are the most important to express, and anything withheld by the client will only compromise their therapy. This whole process is judgement free, and as they engage fully with it, so they will derive maximum benefit from it.

How long does the process take, and how does the therapist know when it is over?

For a start, it is important that the therapist does not make any predictions about this at the beginning of the process. This is because a client in a therapy room is potentially already in a suggestible state, and any predictions the therapist makes might adversely affect the likelihood of the process continuing to a natural conclusion. It is also the case that unless the therapist really is a mind reader, he has no way of knowing how long the process will take. I had a client once who, from the problems she described, I might have predicted would need between eight and twelve sessions. As it happened, she had three major abreactions in her first session, and never needed to come back. She has been in touch with me since, and her life has changed considerably for the better.

As the process draws towards completion, the client should already be feeling significantly unburdened. They will tend to be having less dramatic dreams at night, and their recollections under hypnosis will tend to be less about specific events and more about opinions and general observations. Like many hypno-analysts, I often use a skin resistance meter clipped to my client's fingers to assess their level of emotional arousal under hypnosis. This meter gives a visual indication of their emotional stress level by measuring tiny changes in skin conductivity caused by our tendency to sweat more when our adrenaline rises. If I steer the client's recollections towards previously described traumatic events, they display no emotional arousal when they revisit them in their mind. The recognition that therapy is coming to an end is usually a mutual realisation. In my experience it rarely goes beyond ten or twelve sessions, but is frequently completed in half that time, or less.

I had a client recently, who in her last session visualised a whole group of relatives together, 'in a warm place, free of pain'. She was deeply hypnotised, and I realised straight away that because of the age differences - their lives did not all coincide – she was seeing, or at least imagining, that they had all come together peacefully in the afterlife.

What is subconscious resistance to change, and why does it exist?

As has been previously stated, the fundamental purpose of the subconscious mind is to help to ensure our survival. One of the ways that it attempts to do this is to learn lessons from our life so far, so that we can almost instinctively avoid situations that have previously proven to be unpleasant or threatening. However, some of these lessons are not always logical or helpful in reality. For instance, if a child experienced an unpleasant bout of food poisoning while on a train, the child may develop a phobia of train journeys. The subconscious mind has put a strategy in place that it thinks will provide protection from the perceived threat, and for that reason, it will not be in a rush to release it. It is worth mentioning that it is not uncommon for the strategy to appear years, or even decades, after the sensitising event. So the symptoms may not manifest themselves for 20 or 30 years, when the child has become an adult who commutes. The adult then seeks help from a therapist to resolve the problem.

At this point, the conscious and subconscious minds have different agendas. The conscious mind wants the symptom removed because it is illogical and extremely inconvenient, but the subconscious mind wants to retain it because it views it as a survival strategy. The subconscious mind could therefore put resistance strategies in place which might include, for example, difficulty in recall, and the therapist may encounter a succession of Secondary Sensitising Events or 'screen memories' before the client gets to the real issue. A screen memory is a recollection which may be inaccurate or over-emphasised and it actually masks a different memory which may be more painful or have deeper emotional significance.

It bears repeating that, as a general principle, what we are familiar with has obviously not killed us yet, but change implies unfamiliarity and uncertainty, and therefore potential risk. So we should not be too surprised if the default position of the subconscious mind is to resist change. This characteristic is actually behind one of our biggest behavioural problems – our tendency to be attracted to what is familiar, whether we consciously want it or not. This explains, for example, the inclination of some people to be attracted to the 'wrong' type of partner, and to keep doing it however unpleasant the consequences. This behaviour is what psychologists refer to as 'the urge to repeat'.

How does the therapeutic process actually work?

The release of neurosis is achieved by the client experiencing a full and unhindered abreaction. In Direct Regression to Cause (DRC) therapy, the therapist leads them to this point, and in Free Association, the subconscious mind ends up in the same place, but by a less obvious route. Either way, the client experiences a revivification of the traumatising event. This does not actually mean that they think it is happening again, but the experience is much more real than a memory would be if they were not in a trance state. They will frequently remember more detail, and more crucially, they will also re-experience the emotions they felt at the time to a significant extent. It should be noted that abreaction can occasionally occur spontaneously, and out of trance. Where the trauma has been cumulative, each sensitising event which is revisited will gradually release the neurosis, but where there is a single Initial Sensitising Event (ISE), the neurosis would be released at the point that the ISE is revivified.

So, having possibly recalled a series of Secondary Sensitising Events (SSE's), the client exposes a repressed event, with all the attendant details and emotions. Their physical reaction to this will depend largely on their Warrior/Settler/Nomad status, but even with the reserved Warrior, the observant therapist will spot what is happening. The Settler will usually be obviously upset and tearful, and the Nomad's reaction can often be very dramatic. It is worth noting that analysis is less likely than DRC to run through a series of SSEs before reaching the ISE.

It is essential at this point that the therapist does not become alarmed and feel tempted to take the client to a safe place in their mind, or in fact seek to comfort them in any way, especially physically. The client should be encouraged to engage fully with the experience, describing it in as much detail as possible, however emotional they appear. When the recall of the incident is complete, the therapist asks them to run through it again, giving more physical and emotional detail if possible. Ultimately, the descriptions will become emotion-free, and the client could even end up expressing signs of boredom; at this point, the neurosis will have been fully discharged. The client will often describe feelings of lightness and euphoria at this time, happy to have been released from a burden they have probably been carrying unknowingly since childhood.

A personal example

When I was about four years old, I was playing in our garden and a black Labrador appeared from nowhere and ran towards me. I knew that my Mum was very scared of dogs, and I consequently learned to fear them too. So I ran like hell, and just made it into the kitchen, shutting the door behind me. I have always thought that I remembered this incident clearly, and I have also always thought that it explained why, until very recently, I really disliked black Labradors. They didn't frighten me, but I really disliked them and asked friends who owned them to leave them at home when they visited. I just could not relax with one in the room.

I have already mentioned that I had to go through a process known as training analysis as part of the qualification process to become a therapist. This involves an experienced therapist delving into every possible neurosis or piece of quirky behaviour that they can find. When my issue with Labradors arose, we decided to hypno-analyse it.

Under hypnosis, I remembered the incident in more detail, and the really significant part was completely missing from my conscious recollection of the incident. When I got safely into the kitchen, my Mum, who had seen exactly what had happened, told me that I should not have been scared, and that the dog probably just wanted to play. She was attempting to teach me not to have the fear that she had, but I felt humiliated, as if she were calling me a coward. Under hypnosis, I didn't just remember what she said, I felt the humiliation and expressed it to my therapist. When she asked me to repeat the story, all the details were there, but the feeling had gone. At this point the therapist knew that the trapped emotion had been released.

Very soon afterwards, a friend of mine with a black Labrador came to visit, and I asked her to bring it. It jumped all over me, and I could not have been less concerned. Re-experiencing the 'sensitising event' under hypnosis, with its attendant emotions, had effectively dismantled the neurosis. This is a very simple example, but the process is the same whatever the event being recalled.

Case study – John

John was referred to me by another therapist who had been unable to make any progress resolving what at first appeared to be a strange and completely illogical phobia. John was genuinely terrified of going beyond the second floor of any building. I say 'illogical' because he did not have a fear of heights – on skiing holidays, he would happily dangle from chairlifts which were much further from the ground. This phobia caused him real problems because he worked in London and could not attend client meetings or stay in hotels above the second floor.

As soon as I hypnotised him, he said, in a very surprised voice, "Oh my God – I have just remembered about my brother having his finger amputated!" Until this point, his subconscious mind had completely screened this traumatic incident from his conscious recall. With a little coaxing from me, the full story emerged. His parents had divorced and his father had gone to live in a third floor flat, the front door of which was accessed from an external balcony. One day John and his brother and sister had been playing in the communal garden when they decided to go indoors. The boys chased their sister up the stairs and along the balcony, with John at the back. As his sister went in through the front door of his father's flat, she swung it shut behind her to slow the boys down. His brother put his hand out to try and keep the door open, but it shut on his finger and actually amputated it. Being behind his brother, John did not actually see what had happened, but suddenly his brother was screaming in agony, with blood going everywhere.

At times of danger, our subconscious minds are desperate to learn lessons to keep us safe in future. The only feature of the scene in front of John which could be interpreted as a threat was the height as he looked over the balcony, and this became established in his subconscious as a situation to avoid at all costs in future. Hence his somewhat unusual phobia.

While he was still in hypnosis, I rationalised what had happened, and used some Cognitive Behavioural Therapy (CBT) before bringing him 'back into the room'. This one session completely resolved the issue, and a few days later he emailed me a photograph he had taken from 19 floors up in an office block – looking out across the rooftops to the London Eye. Problem solved.

A more dramatic example

Quite recently, I had a client who came to me because she was being very unforgiving and vocalising a high level of anger within her relationship. You will remember that when inappropriate emotions are expressed, or emotions are expressed to an inappropriate extent, what is actually happening is that the emotion being vented is unresolved, or trapped, from a previous event. Consciously, she had no idea what this was.

Under hypnosis, she told me that she had a pony as a child which she absolutely loved, and she spent all her free time after school and at weekends looking after it. When she was about twelve, it was diagnosed with cancer and had to be put down. She groomed it for the last time, and the vet came to put it to sleep by lethal injection, or so she thought. What actually happened was that the vet shot the pony *while she had her arms around it!*

Unsurprisingly, she was in floods of tears while she recounted what had happened, and she was still upset when she told me the story for the second time. On the third time of telling, she gave me more detail, but the emotion was gone.

She recently told me that her relationship issues largely resolved themselves after this session, and that she and her partner were getting on very much better. She was able to let things go in a way that she had never previously been able to.

Chapter 9

The art of self-hypnosis

How to hypnotise yourself

If you can master the art of hypnotising yourself, you have literally gained the ability to re-program your subconscious mind at will. But please bear in mind what I have said all along about needing to uninstal negative programs before you instal positive ones. This is why I have listed this skill after hypno-analysis.

It took me nearly a year, and several books, to figure out how to hypnotise myself. Do not let this put you off however, because my difficulties were caused by the fact that I am quite 'resistant'. This means that no one else, even a professional therapist, can hypnotise me easily either. In truth, when I figured it out, I realised that self-hypnosis really isn't that difficult. I can now achieve the state at will, given a comfortable quiet environment. I didn't find any of the books particularly helpful, so I will explain how I would approach the matter now.

Before I do, let me answer a question which worries a lot of people – can you get 'stuck' in hypnosis if you hypnotise yourself? Any book on hypnosis will tell you that you can't. The truth of the matter is that if you are genuinely unable to rouse yourself from the trance state, you will ultimately fall asleep, and then in due course, you will wake up naturally into a normal waking state.

I have on several occasions hypnotised myself extremely deeply, and have not found it easy to come out of it. I ended up with one part of my mind saying, 'It's time to get back to reality', and another part saying, 'I'm staying here - I'm extremely happy where I am'. But I have always succeeded in rousing myself. It is as if you know you ought to be doing something, but you really, really can't be bothered. I have never been in this situation for more than an hour, and I now have strategies that stop this happening. If you can physically move, it helps enormously in breaking the spell, but because you are so deeply relaxed, moving is really not easy. When I go really deep, I literally cannot lift my hands - they feel like lead - but I have found that I can wiggle them sideways, and once you move a bit, the rest comes easily.

I really don't want to put you off trying this, but I am just being honest. You are very unlikely to go this deep initially, and as you get better at going deeper, so you become more at ease with the whole process and more relaxed about getting out of it again. As well as giving me the opportunity to instal any subconscious programs that I want, I find it deeply, deeply relaxing. It also provides an excellent way of talking to my 'inner child'.

Before we discuss how to get into the trance state, you need to know how to get out!

Getting into the trance state is achieved by 'self-talk', and so is getting out. When you want to come out of it, tell yourself that you can count yourself back to reality using the numbers one to five – something along these lines should work well:

One – just beginning to be aware of your body again now.

Two – being aware of how powerful and relaxed you now feel.

Three – being aware of any sounds, inside or outside the room.

Four – just beginning to move your finger and toes, and…

Five – opening your eyes and feeling fantastic.

If this doesn't bring you right out, do it again. As explained above, if I go really deep, wiggling my hands sideways helps to make me more aware of my surroundings because it begins to re-connect me with my physical environment, and I then know that I can rouse myself. Make sure that you do not immediately drive or put yourself into any potentially dangerous situation, until you feel 100% present. This may take a little time.

Here are some pre-requisites which I consider fundamentally important for beginners:

1. You need to be as physically comfortable as you can possibly get. I sit up on my bed with plenty of pillows behind me. I find if I lie down, I am more likely to go to sleep.

2. You need to be free from any distractions. By that I mean that you need to know for certain that you will not be disturbed, so switch the phone off, disconnect the doorbell if you can't get out of earshot of it. Ask anyone else in the house to be quiet and leave you in peace. No pets in the room obviously. Although I am lucky enough to live somewhere quiet, I also use noise reducing headphones to further reduce distractions. The less that any of your senses are triggered by your environment, the easier it is to leave that environment behind.

3. It is important that you are not tired – if you are, you will be likely to fall asleep whatever posture you adopt.

4. It is also important that you are not highly stressed, or have specific concerns on your mind. It will be much harder to 'let go' of reality if insistent thoughts keep popping into your head. Writing them down before you start might help. If any unwanted thoughts intrude while I am hypnotising myself, I visualise putting them into a helium balloon and watching them float away from me. Different things work for different people – maybe you could see yourself in a Monty Python-esque cartoon,

with your skull opening and your unwanted thought being released. In truth, if I know that I am preoccupied with a particular problem, I don't even try to hypnotise myself until I have resolved it, or at least shelved it effectively.

Absolute silence and lack of distractions are recommended, but not essential once you have succeeded in mastering the process. I once hypnotised myself very deeply while sitting outside in a deckchair, with cars going past and planes flying overhead. It is simply that the more optimal the conditions, the quicker and easier it is likely to be. One more thing – the old adage, 'If at first you don't succeed, try, try, try again' is certainly wise advice.

The direct method

This method simply relies on 'self-talk' and is deceptively simple. If your lifestyle permits, try and do this when you have no time constraints. If you have to set an alarm, it is hard not to start wondering how soon the alarm will go off. Begin with the conscious intention of doing nothing more than getting extremely comfortable, and extremely relaxed. It is quite helpful to go through a checklist of body parts, making sure that there is no residual tension in any area of your body. I find that as I relax, my arms and legs feel heavier. Maybe visualise breathing in calmness and breathing out stress.

By 'self-talk', I mean talking to yourself in your head, with suggestions such as, 'With every breath I take, I sink deeper and deeper into a trance state', or 'Every time I swallow (which is autonomic and happens unconsciously), I go five times deeper'. You will notice that the statements are in the present tense. Allow time for them to happen. When my arms and legs feel heavier, I tell myself that the extra weight will allow me to sink faster and faster into a deeper and deeper state of relaxation. After a while, you will realise that you are extremely conscious, but not of your surroundings. The consciousness is completely focussed inwards, and you are then ready to start work.

A very successful American hypnotist by the name of Dave Elman noticed that every week that clients came to see him, they hypnotised more easily. He studied this phenomenon in detail, and eventually reduced the steps required to achieve this into his famous 'Three Minute Induction'. When I read about this, I decided to try it. It took me three minutes to get into trance, and an hour and a half to get out! I slumped forward in my chair, and despite being very uncomfortable, I just couldn't move. It was one of the deepest trances I had ever been in. There are details of this method on the internet, and in his book which is simply called *Hypnotherapy*, but I wouldn't recommend it for beginners just in case it works as well on you as it did on me.[27]

Incidentally, I named my therapy business after a comment Dave Elman made in this book. He described his job as piloting people's dreams, and *The Dream Pilot* is a tribute to him. Hypnosis is a dream-like state, and the hypno-analyst facilitates the client's therapy by piloting their dreams towards the past events that triggered their problems in the first place.

The indirect method

Before I describe this method, it is helpful to work out your natural modality, in other words whether you are primarily a 'Visual', 'Auditory' or 'Kinaesthetic' person. Any professional therapist who knows what they are doing will work this out about their clients because it makes it easier to hypnotise them. Visual people are more concerned with what things look like than what they sound or feel like, and will describe things primarily in a visual way. They will also use visual metaphors such as 'I see what you mean'. Auditory people are much more interested in sound and will use metaphors such as 'I hear you'. Kinaesthetic people are much more concerned with how things feel – they are much more inclined to describe textures, and to say, 'I really feel for you'.

I am definitely kinaesthetic – for example when I buy clothes I am much more concerned with what they feel like to wear than what they look like on me. The relevance of this knowledge is that when you hypnotise yourself, using the indirect 'daydreaming method', you will find that by filling your visualisation with plenty of details that match your personal modality, you will detach from reality much more easily.

So, you are ready to start. All the same rules apply about getting as comfortable and relaxed as possible, with no possible distractions. Your conscious intention is to get into a very realistic daydream, in other words, to distract yourself from your current reality. Visualise yourself in a really relaxing situation – let us use the example of lying on a beach in the Caribbean. Use all of your senses, but make sure you use plenty that match your modality. If you are primarily visual, picture the sunshine being reflected off the sea and the fronds of palm trees waving in the gentle breeze. If you are auditory, listen to the rhythmic sounds of the surf on the beach, and the faint cries of seabirds. If you are kinaesthetic, feel the warmth of the sun on your skin, and the sand underneath you.

This may or may not be a useful piece of advice, but don't make the mistake of trying too hard – just relax and let it happen. You can include self-talk in this method - tell yourself that every breath you take makes the visualisation more real. Feel the sun on your limbs as they get heavier, listen to the sounds as you relax more and more deeply.

So what is the difference between daydreaming and being hypnotised? Nothing – they are one and the same thing. Once you can detach from reality and become 100% involved in your daydream, you can remain in that deeply relaxed state while you alter your focus and go deeper. As soon as you are aware of that detachment from the reality of your room, count backwards, really slowly, telling yourself that each number takes you deeper and deeper. As you feel yourself going deeper, visualise every step on a long staircase that takes you down and down and down.

The daydreaming part is known as a 'hypnotic induction' and the counting process is referred to as a deepener. When you feel totally detached from reality, you are ready to start work.

What 'work' can you do under hypnosis?

You can do one of two things.

a)   You can work on yourself in your own mind, doing inner child work for instance, or visualising what you want in the future. Because you are in a hypnotic state, you have drawn your Conscious Critical Faculty aside, and can instal new programs and new core beliefs direct into your subconscious mind. In this state, you are highly suggestible to your own 'self-talk' and visualisations. For example, there are many reports of people making highly significant improvements to their health through self-hypnosis, totally confounding medical expectation.

b) You can listen to recordings that you have bought or made previously that instal carefully worded messages, played on a loop if you like. I can't emphasise enough that the messages need to be carefully thought out, and positive in every way, otherwise you could end up acheiving the opposite effect to that which you desire. You cannot say, for example, 'I do not like alcohol' or 'I am not a smoker' – the subconscious mind does not recognise negative concepts, so actually takes in the *opposite* message – in this case 'I do like alcohol' and 'I am a smoker'.

If, having hypnotised yourself, you wish to play a pre-recorded script from your tablet or phone, you will not suddenly come out of the trance if you open your eyes for five seconds to press the 'play' button. Before you do so, just tell yourself that you will stay deeply relaxed as you do it, and you will. You are, of course, in a highly suggestible state at this point, so what you tell yourself will happen, does happen.

How do you know if you were hypnotised?

When you are ready to come out of the trance state, you count yourself back out. If you are unsure whether you succeeded in hypnotising yourself on this occasion, here are a few clues:

1. When you opened your eyes, did you have any sense at all of being momentarily surprised at finding yourself back in the room? If so, you were hypnotised.
2. Without looking at a clock, guess how long you were in the trance state. If, when you check the time, you seriously underestimated the elapsed time (this is known as time distortion), you were probably hypnotised.
3. If at any time in your daydream it was sufficiently realistic that you forgot where you actually were, you were hypnotised.

You will remember from the last chapter that a good definition of the state of hypnosis is that it is a state of Effortless Selective Thinking. In this case, it would mean that you were 100% involved in your daydream or trance, and consequently 0% involved in your current reality – sitting on your bed. A lot of hypnotherapists' clients deny that they were hypnotised, not because they weren't, but because they didn't recognise the hypnotic state. The fact that they heard everything that the therapist said to them during the session does not for one minute mean that they weren't hypnotised – it is more likely to mean the opposite because their attention didn't wander.

My own hypnotic visualisation

Over the time that I have been doing this, I have developed a complex and sophisticated visualisation that I regularly use. It goes like this.

I am walking down a path towards a castle, and I go in through a pair of large wooden doors. I walk into the main hall, and there is a large inglenook fireplace, big enough to stand in. I move a concealed handle in the fireplace, and a secret door opens. I go through it and close the door behind me. There is a dimly lit spiral staircase with twenty stone steps. I count them down as I descend, from twenty to one. The symbolism here is of course that being underground represents descending into my subconscious mind.

I find myself in a large hall, with three archways leading into various rooms. The room on the left has a massive security door on it, like a walk-in safe, and only I know the combination. Behind that door is a control room where I can adjust every possible parameter about myself – from my energy levels to my intelligence. When I leave it, I always make sure the door is securely locked.

On the opposite side of the hall is a huge room where all my memories are stored. The filing cabinets are in rows, a row for each year, with a gap down the middle of the room. I can go to any year, and search for memories from that period of my life.

The third archway leads to a large room with a stone therapy table that I can lie on. There are huge coloured crystals in the ceiling that can be moved so that coloured, healing sunlight shines directly onto me – red for my circulation system, blue for my nervous system, green for my digestive system, etc. If I think my body needs a tune up, I go and get one!

Off to the side of the room is a smaller one where I can meet my soul mates and talk with them – people like my beloved grandfather. This is also where I do my inner child work. I also have a point where I can leave my body and just travel with my mind, but that is another story! If you don't think I am completely mad at this point, you never will, but I find this an incredibly profound way of optimising my mind and body.

Chapter 10

The surprising sources of our deeper instincts, drives and feelings

The influence of our ancestors

You may never have thought about this, but it is undoubtedly true that a significant amount of our subconscious behaviour is not driven by our past experiences, but by the experiences of our ancestors. Consider this scenario from when I was a tree surgeon.

It was a peaceful, sunny afternoon at an English vicarage where I was working with two colleagues. Suddenly, an agonised yell of pain split the summer air. Phil and I looked up to see that the vicar's donkey had bitten Ian on the buttock. He was now sprinting for the fence, closely followed by the donkey which was clearly anxious to repeat the experience. As far as I know, donkeys are not carnivores, so it was Ian's dignity, not his life, which was at stake. Phil and I were instantly helpless with laughter - we laughed so much that it hurt as Ian cleared the fence in the nick of time. He immediately dropped his trousers to examine his wounded butt cheek. Donkeys have large protruding teeth, and the bite must have been extremely painful, but Phil and I were completely unable to offer anything but endless roars of laughter. Even the donkey joined in, cantering around the field repeating the bizarre 'eeyore' noise that donkeys make. Ian however, was much more eloquent - I have never heard such a long string of heartfelt expletives that avoided hesitation or repetition. I sincerely hope the vicar wasn't in earshot. Phil and I hadn't laughed so much for weeks - there was absolutely no prospect at all that Ian was going to hear a single word of concern or sympathy from us - we just laughed until it hurt.

Why do people behave like this? Human behaviour fascinates me - so much of it is so instinctive, so deeply rooted in our past, that we neither notice nor question it. I once read somewhere that laughter is an instinctive communication to tell the rest of your tribe that danger has passed. This makes perfect sense in the scenario described above - Ian was being assaulted by a potentially dangerous animal, but Phil and I figured that he would almost certainly survive, so the hoots of laughter that accompanied his sprint across the field were really just Phil and I celebrating his survival. Interestingly, this theory also explains why some people find slapstick comedy so funny – the viewer is presented with an almost continual stream of events where people appear to be getting hurt, but he knows that they are not.

I mention this story because it is an example of how important it is to bear in mind that much of our behaviour is deeply ingrained in us by tens of thousands of years of human history. There is no possible benefit to 'our tribe' these days in laughing at the scenario I described above - but we still do it, and we don't question it. Human beings are immensely complex on an emotional, psychological and physical level, and to begin to understand our own behaviour, or that of others, we frequently need to look at it in the context of a much wider range of issues, from microbiology, symbiosis and tens of thousands of years of human evolution. In this chapter, I want to examine some of the more bizarre factors that influence the way we behave and feel.

A different way to reduce the conflict between our conscious and subconscious wishes

So far in this book, I have suggested ways that we might identify and change some of our subconscious programs so that there is less inconsistency between our conscious and subconscious wishes. The more closely aligned our instinctive subconsciously-driven behaviour is with our conscious wishes, the happier we will be, and the more successful will be our relationships. But there is a completely different way that we can endeavour to achieve this harmony. This is to understand our deeply held human instincts and, wherever possible, choose a lifestyle that complements, rather than conflicts with, that human history. In a very real sense, this feeds the soul.

For example, my house is made from natural materials such as wood and stone, and it contains the absolute minimum of plastic. I hunt my own food wherever possible, (excluding the fruit and vegetables of course!) and I sometimes forage for natural food such as edible fungi. I heat the house by log fire rather than using fossil fuels. I have made my own furniture from trees I have cut down. In my mind, these behaviours are in harmony with deeply held instincts, and consequently I find that living in compliance with them is deeply satisfying.

In winter, the first thing I do when I get up in the morning is to rake through the ashes of the previous night's fire to see if there are any embers that could conceivably be coaxed back into life. If there are, I will spend ten minutes blowing on them to relight the fire rather than using a match and a sheet of newspaper. Why do I do this? It's simple - for most of human history we had no matches, and if you let the fire go out, it was extremely hard to light it again. I know this because I have used a stick and bow to light a fire. It is extremely difficult, frustrating and time-consuming. Correspondingly, it is extremely satisfying to rekindle a fire from yesterday's embers, and I recognise that this pleasure is still deeply wired into my psyche today.

Think about people's favourite rural pastimes, and their deeper connections. We love walking in the country – as we would if we were foraging for food centuries ago. Fishing, a really popular relaxing pastime, reminds us of times when this was how families got essential high protein food from water. Many of us enjoy having barbecues – cooking over an open fire, even though we have access to other quicker and cleaner fuels, invokes deep hunter-gatherer instincts. Growing plants in our garden that we can eat, not just look at, even though they are widely available in supermarkets, gives us a real sense of health and pride in our own efforts. Walking the dog these days is a pleasure; in the past, hunting dogs helped us to locate and catch animals to eat. Horse riding – no longer the only mode of transport but still we enjoy hugely the connection with horses and the sensation of being close to nature when we are with them, and perhaps we forget that they have helped us to fight our enemies and till the land for thousands of years. It really is not hard to see that we are deeply wedded to the activities in our past that helped to sustain us.

In the appendix that follows, I talk about alcohol, and refer to the fact that tastes and smells are pleasant or unpleasant depending on whether the source of them is good for us or bad for us. However, there is another reason that we like or dislike certain smells – the deeply held connotations they have in our minds. Think about wood smoke – most people like this smell, although it could not in truth be described as good for us. However, think about how many thousands of years our ancestors would have experienced trudging back to their settlements, tired, cold and hungry, carrying the woolly mammoth they had just trapped. As soon as they could smell wood smoke, they knew that they were nearly home, and that their 'womenfolk' had got the fire alight. They would soon be warmed up, dried out and tucking into a hot, juicy, medium-rare mammoth burger. Why wouldn't they like the smell of wood smoke?

Think about fire more generally: many people, from small boys to grown-ups, are fascinated by fire. I certainly was – remember I nearly burned our house down once! This fascination is not without reason. When humans mastered fire, it was a huge turning point for the human race – here are a few reasons why:

1. They could cook food thereby deriving far more goodness from it, which meant that they had to spend far less time hunting, gathering and eating.
2. They could use it to scare away wild animals and keep themselves safe.
3. It allowed them to keep warm in cold climates, and therefore populate a much wider geographical range.
4. They could use it to clear vast areas of vegetation to grow crops more easily.
5. They ultimately learned to use it to smelt metal ores and make metal tools, weapons and armour.

No wonder we are still fascinated by it. I am just as happy sitting and looking into the fire as I am watching television. If I had a choice between living in a well-appointed, centrally-heated flat in a city, or a rustic caravan with a woodstove, I would choose the caravan every time. Absolutely no question – I know what feeds my soul.

When I see football hooliganism on the news, I see groups of men exercising their instinctive need to indulge in tribal behaviour. They get together with other members of their tribe of fighting age and have a confrontation with a neighbouring tribe – just as their ancestors did for thousands of years. Why is it predominantly men who go fishing? Literally millions of British men regularly choose to go and sit on a cold wet riverbank, in the hope of catching some fish that they can't eat. Why do they do it? Because it fulfils an instinctive need to know that they still have the skills to catch food and potentially provide for their family. Using your debit card to pay the bill at Sainsbury's supermarket is too far removed from this reality to feed their soul in the same way.

Knowledge of our anthropological background is unquestionably interesting, and helps us to live in harmony with our deepest instincts. But it can also help us to make sense of our present day behaviour. Consider the subject of trying to lose weight - an issue which affects millions of people. For evolutionary reasons, we instinctively gorge on sweet food. For thousands of years, there was a clear advantage to doing this. If, as a forager, you came upon a tree laden with ripe oranges, this provided a plentiful source of cheap energy. If, being mindful of your figure, you ate just one, planning to return the following day for another, you ran the risk of other humans or animals having stripped the tree bare in the interim. It would have made much better sense from the perspective of survival to eat as many oranges as you could at the first opportunity, and again at any later opportunity if it arose. In fact, when fruit is plentiful (in the autumn), it made perfect sense to put on weight in preparation for the inevitable scarcity of food in winter. There is some evidence to suggest that fructose, the sugar found in fruit, actually triggers us to put on weight for this evolutionary reason. Fructose is a cheap form of sugar which is widely used in processed foods which we eat all year round – it would not be surprising if this is not contributing to the current obesity epidemic in the West.

In the affluent western world, both fruit and sweet food are also abundant all year round and we clearly have an evolutionary instinct to gorge on it when it is available. This does not entirely explain why so many people are overweight, because, by this logic, everyone would be overweight, but it is certainly 'food for thought'. We clearly now need to consciously resist the instinct to overeat sweet food because it no longer has the biological advantage that it used to have. Lack of access to energy-rich food no longer threatens our survival in the way that it has previously done. In fact, more people in the world are now overweight than underweight.

Interestingly, as with any compulsive behaviour, overeating is another situation where we have to suspect that the subconscious mind may also be playing a part, of which the conscious mind is totally unaware. If we frequently eat more than we consciously wish to, it is a fair assumption that at some level, the subconscious mind sees some advantage in our being overweight but which we do not consciously understand. There could be a wide variety of reasons for this, but as a therapist, I have more than once noticed overweight clients who have been subjected to abusive situations in their past which might have triggered this reaction. Maybe their subconscious mind has decided that it would be an advantage not to be an overtly 'sexual' shape, maybe they are creating a physical barrier between 'themselves' and 'others'. This is undoubtedly a complex subject, and there are obviously many other possible reasons for weight gain - some related to abuse, but many not.

The symbiotic relationships we have developed with bacteria

In Chapter 7, I explained that we can control our feelings by controlling our thoughts, and while this is true, there are other factors which also affect the way we feel. Over the course of human history, we have developed an increasingly complex symbiotic relationship with our gut bacteria. These bacteria have learned to produce neurotransmitters, such as dopamine and serotonin, which directly affect our moods.

Specifically, dopamine regulates our responses to things which give us pleasure and affects our reactions to them. Serotonin directly affects our feelings of happiness. Like every other type of organism on the planet, bacteria want to increase their numbers and propagate themselves as widely as possible. If they could make us crave specific foods that are good for them (but not necessarily for us), their numbers in our gut would multiply. There are no prizes for guessing that they can make you crave what they want, not what you want. Maybe you don't actually like chocolate at all, but your gut flora is addicted to Green and Black's? Food for thought! If the bacteria are then able to make us happier, we are likely to be more sociable, and if we are more sociable we will be likely to be in closer contact with other humans, and consequently be more likely to spread our gut bacteria to them. It is fair to assume that personal hygiene was probably not as big an issue for most of our history as it is today.

In her fascinating book *The Molecules of Emotion*, Dr Candace Pert explains that various organs in our bodies, especially our gut, are littered with receptors for these neurotransmitters.[28] When we want to know someone's deep, instinctive reaction to something, rather than asking for their cerebral response, we ask people what their gut feeling is. Your gut really does have feelings! If you believed that your feelings were solely generated by the thoughts in your head, this is far from being the case. The upshot of this discovery is that our moods and cravings are, to a large extent, at the mercy of billions of gut bacteria over which we have no control at all! Or do we?

The understanding that the microbiome in our gut can potentially be responsible for our general level of happiness has led to a possible treatment for chronic depression which goes by the name of Faecal Microbiota Transplant. If you are of a sensitive nature, or are about to eat, skip the next two paragraphs! The treatment involves introducing into your digestive system a stool sample from a person who is by nature cheerful and optimistic. This sample is put in a food liquidiser with an appropriate amount of water to form a stool smoothie. (Note 1 – make absolutely sure that the lid is on tight! Note 2 – withdraw the liquidiser from service after this procedure).

The next problem you have is successfully introducing this faecal solution into your own gut – and the good news is that you don't have to take it orally. The accepted way of doing this involves a plastic bag, a length of tubing and gravity. I will leave the exact details to your imagination. It has been widely reported that depressed recipients of faecal transplants have frequently demonstrated significant and lasting improvements to their mood. Improvements in many other conditions, such as allergies, have also been recorded.

There are details of the whole process on the internet, but I do not for one minute recommend that you try this at home. It is a medical procedure and should be done under medical supervision. One of the reasons for this is the possibility of infecting yourself with the stool donor's parasites. The next section explains one of the potential adverse consequences of doing this.

Can parasites and viruses also affect our moods and behaviour?

In a word, yes - this somewhat alarming concept seems likely to be true. The microscopic cat parasite Toxoplasma gondii is a fascinating example. When it gets into a rat, it has been demonstrated to make host rats three times more likely to take risks than uninfected ones. It also changes their attitude towards feline urine, making them attracted to it, rather than repelled by it.[29] The rat's natural repulsion to cat urine has the obvious biological advantage of keeping them out of their predator's territory. What drives the parasite to change the behaviour of the rat is that while the parasite can live happily in the rat, it can only reproduce in a feline host. So the biological advantage to the parasite is that the changed behaviour of the rat makes it much more likely to get eaten by a cat, and this enables the parasite to get back into a host where it can multiply.

It turns out that chimpanzees can also get this parasite, and it has exactly the same effect on their behaviour. Their natural predator is the leopard, and infected chimps are much less likely to run for the trees when they see a leopard. Their ability to conduct sensible risk assessments has been severely compromised, and they are consequently much more likely to get eaten by leopards, thereby returning the parasite to a host that allows it to reproduce.

So what has this got to do with humans? A lot, as it happens. I read an article in The Week magazine which reported that up to 60% of the human population also hosts this parasite – could this explain why so many people like cats, which (unlike dogs) are pretty useless to humans? No offence intended here – I like cats – but our relationship with them makes little sense in evolutionary terms. For tens of thousands of years, we have had a symbiotic relationship with dogs. They have helped us to locate, track and catch prey, to tend our flocks of domestic animals and alerted us to potential predators and helped protect us from them. In return, we have housed, fed and looked after them. Cats on the other hand have never been anything to us except predators. Have they actually learned to spread this parasite to us so that we like and look after them rather than hate and fear them? If this parasite can affect the behaviour of such a close relative of ours as the chimp, it is not beyond the realms of possibility. And if they can do this, can they also affect our perception of, and reaction to, risk? Do cat owners have a higher incidence of motor vehicle accidents? Should they pay higher car insurance premiums? I have absolutely no idea, but it would be an interesting question to research.

The possibility of such a tiny organism taking some degree of control over a host the size of a human should not surprise us – think about the rabies virus. Rabies changes the personality of its host by making it more aggressive, stimulating an excess supply of virus-infected saliva and then making it want to bite other animals. Aggressive biting, to some extent, is natural behaviour in dogs, but not in humans. How does a virus make a human suddenly feel like biting other humans and animals? You have to go back a very long way into our history to find a time when we would have done this. Is the virus triggering some very deeply buried human instinct, or has it found a way to create an entirely new pattern of behaviour in us? Either way, it is a remarkable achievement. Just how remarkable becomes clear when you consider that the ratio of size between a virus and a human being is about the same as the ratio of size of a human being and planet Earth!

Further reading on the subject of anthropology

The more you study issues such as these, the more unbelievably complex human behaviour appears. Anthropology is the study of human development since the arrival of Homo sapiens on planet Earth around 100,000 years ago. By this point, you will have realised that only a small percentage of our behaviour is truly within the control of our conscious minds The majority is either controlled by our subconscious mind or by microorganisms. Of the subconsciously controlled areas, a significant number can be traced back to deeply-wired instincts which were installed many thousands of years ago. These deeply held instincts are far easier to make sense of when they are viewed in the context of the way that humans have mostly lived over that period. It goes without saying that it is far easier to make an effort to live in harmony with them than it is to try and change them.

Civilisation as we know it is a very recent phenomenon, and the majority of our instincts go back much, much further. Statistically, 85% of our last 100,000 years has been spent as hunter-gatherers – that is to say, it was pre the Agricultural Revolution when we began to grow crops and domesticate animals. If the subject of anthropology interests you, I would recommend reading *Sapiens: A Brief History of Humankind* by Yuval Noah Harari.[30] He offers fascinating, surprising and well-argued perspectives on a wide variety of events in human history, and in doing so, he makes sense of much of our instinctive behaviour today.

Conclusion

I would not claim that every person who has an emotional or behavioural problem has acquired it in the ways that I have described in this book. For instance, clearly if it is possible to inherit memory - which seems extremely likely - it is also highly likely that we could inherit behaviour patterns. It would certainly be biologically advantageous if we could, because we would be born with pre-programmed adaptations to our parents' environment and circumstances, and hence our own environment and circumstances. It is also very likely that events that occurred to the mother during pregnancy, or a traumatic birth for example, could have ongoing adverse effects on our psychological wellbeing.

However, what I can claim is that this is not true for the vast majority of the clients that I see in my therapy room. In almost every case that I come across, people do not say that they have always had the problem. Instead, they are much more likely to say that they never used to be like this, but that at some point in their life, their feelings and behaviour changed. Sometimes it happened gradually, and sometimes quite suddenly, but they are almost always aware that a change occurred.

The timing of the change does not always help us to pinpoint the cause, because the change may have occurred as the result of a

Secondary Sensitising Event, whereas of course the real problem was an Initial Sensitising Event which they may, or may not, remember. I have never conducted a statistical analysis of client data, but I would estimate that in at least 80% of cases, the events that induced the client's trauma occurred before the age of eighteen. There are several reasons why this should not surprise us:

1. Our subconscious mind is designed to be much more easily programmable when we are younger, because we have a lot to learn in a relatively short time. The Conscious Critical Faculty does not start to form until around the age of three and is not fully in place until nearing the end of our teens.

2. We frequently deny children the opportunity to express what they are feeling. They may be told, for example, that being angry with their parents is unacceptable, or that they just need to pull themselves together and be brave when they are afraid. So children are more likely to repress emotions than adults, and end up with these emotions trapped at a subconscious level.

3. Children are more easily frightened, and we know that new core beliefs can be installed very easily at times of high emotion such as fear.

I am therefore of the opinion that the vast majority of clients' neuroses amount to *learned behaviour*, and as I have previously said, what has been learned can be unlearned. And by doing so, it should be perfectly possible to become the person that we would have been if the sensitising trauma had never occurred. So how do we permanently divest ourselves of our invisible emotional burden?

Carrying emotional baggage

You often hear people talk about *emotional baggage*. As has already been said, whenever we talk about this subject we refer to people *holding* resentment, *bearing* a grudge, being *burdened* by guilt. We use this language for a reason – it quite correctly implies that we are being weighed down by something.

Let us imagine that you have an invisible rucksack on your back, and all your unresolved emotions get put in it. This rucksack weighs you down, day in and day out, but because it is behind you, you are completely unaware of it. Some people's rucksacks were filled at a young age, and others just keep accumulating extra weight into adulthood. The day-to-day effect of carrying this rucksack is that every time you need to overcome one of the many obstacles that life throws in your path, you have much more difficulty in doing so. Life seems, and indeed is, far more difficult for you than it is for others. You struggle, you get tired and frustrated, you lean excessively on your friends, you get depressed or irritable, maybe you drink excessively or take drugs (medicinal or recreational) to ease the pain. To a greater or lesser extent, this is how many people get through life. Their rucksack may just have one heavy object in it, or it may have several of varying sizes. Its contents are not especially relevant, but the invisible burden is always there.

The metaphorical rucksack, this invisible junk container, is of course a compartment of your subconscious mind. In truth, I think that there are very few people who do not inadvertently carry at least some emotional 'junk' on their journey through life. Given that the rucksack and its contents are invisible, it would make sense to seek the advice and assistance of someone who at least had some specialist knowledge of how to sort through the contents. This is how I see the role of the hypno-analyst.

Getting help sorting through the rucksack

I have mentioned a wide range of therapies and techniques in this book, all of which have helped me in some way or other, but you will already be aware that I think that hypno-analysis stands head and shoulders above all the others – I can only talk from my own experiences. Here are some of the reasons I hold it in such high regard:

1. Hypno-analysis is relatively fast – the average number of times a client sees me is five. More than ten sessions is exceptionally unusual. Sometimes the therapy is extraordinarily fast – I made a house visit to an agoraphobic client once, and at the end of a one-hour session, we went out for a thirty-minute walk – something which she had been unable to do for years. Her subconscious mind went to the source of the problem within about fifteen minutes of the start of the session and she then spent half an hour describing it. I spent fifteen minutes using CBT while she was still hypnotised to re-program her mind with a more rational explanation of what had occurred. The problem which had caused her to lose her job and her partner and suffer numerous panic attacks, was genuinely and fully resolved in one hour.

2. It is highly effective – 80% of my clients achieve results which they describe as an 'excellent' resolution of their presenting issue. These include many potentially difficult problems such as alcoholism and anorexia. Of the remaining 20%, I would say that most are simply not ready to face their issues, or they have a 'secondary gain' which they are, at some level, unwilling or unable to give up. Incidentally, it is for this reason that I never accept referrals from third parties. If a client is ready to address

their problems, they will call me. If they came because a third party had badgered them into seeking help, the outcome would be unlikely to be positive.

3. In my experience the resolution is, almost without exception, permanent. On the very rare occasions that a client comes back for further sessions, it is usually because they chose not to disclose something in their original work with me. Usually, even if clients start off with the intention of withholding deeply personal or traumatic experiences, sooner or later they understand that any lack of disclosure on their part will only inhibit the resolution of their presenting issues.

In truth, at the key points in therapy when they are actually 'unloading' deeply personal and emotional issues, I don't need to hear what they say – they just need to express it. For this reason, I have often suggested that clients do this in their mother tongue if they were born abroad. I have had clients work on unresolved grief by talking to deceased relatives in Russian, Icelandic and Persian, to name just a few. I have absolutely no idea what they said, and it didn't matter in the slightest. This is why hypno-analysts should never think that they have 'fixed' anybody. The client fixes themselves – the therapist just facilitates the process.

4. One of the great advantages of this therapy is that it doesn't involve willpower, and this is really crucial when it comes to breaking habits like alcohol abuse. By now you will know that if you find yourself trying to use your willpower to change your behaviour, what you have actually done is to pick a fight with your subconscious mind. You should also now know how that fight is likely to end! We know that habits, those subconscious shortcuts, are simple programs that prompt us to do 'y' when 'x' happens. Change the program – do 'z' when 'x' happens instead. It really is that simple. I used to run a program that said, 'When you sit down to supper, open a bottle of wine' (and usually finish it). I now run a different program, and it honestly never even occurs to me to open a bottle of wine. I simply don't have even the slightest urge to have wine with my evening meal.

Choosing a hypno-analyst

This chapter is not an advert for my therapy business - the vast majority of people reading this will be geographically too far away for that to be possible. It is, if anything, an advert for the therapeutic power of the hypno-analysis process. It has worked for me personally, and I have seen countless clients make hugely positive changes to their lives in a way that still sometimes amazes me. Other therapies certainly have their place and undoubtedly can be highly effective – I am not suggesting otherwise for one minute. But I speak as I find – my experience as a client and as a therapist is that it can be outstandingly effective, and being a hypno-analyst is without question the most rewarding job I could ever imagine having.

When choosing a therapist, the most important factor by far is how comfortable you feel with them. You should feel an almost instinctive connection with them - that they genuinely care about the outcome of your therapy. You must feel that you would be safe telling them your deepest secrets and be confident that they would not judge you in any way. Therapists refer to this connection as rapport, and the stronger it is, the more effective the therapy is likely to be. For this reason, I offer a free first session, which seeks to achieve four goals:

1. To gather information about the client's issues, and make sure that I think I can help them.
2. To explain the hypno-analysis process, and make sure that they are committed to going through with it.
3. To make sure that we are both happy working with each other – i.e. that we have rapport.
4. To make sure that it is safe to continue, i.e. to check that they are not using recreational drugs, are not pregnant, and to ensure as far as possible that they are not psychotic.

Not all therapists provide a free first session, and they are in no way obliged to, but they should certainly make clear that there is absolutely no obligation to continue if you do not feel comfortable to do so.

My training course was written by Terence Watts of the Essex Institute of Clinical Hypnosis (EICH), and his website - www.essexinstitute.co.uk - has a 'Find a Therapist' page. These would all be people that have completed an EICH course, although not necessarily the same hypno-analysis course that I undertook. If you wish to contact me, you can do so through my website, www.thedreampilot.co.uk, or by email: thedreampilot@sky.com

Your journey

In my opinion, the therapeutic journey has no ending – there is always work we can do to improve our emotional and physical wellbeing, the quality of our relationships and our interactions with others.

Thank you for taking an interest in the somewhat tortuous path I took before I figured out what was happening in my chaotic life. I hope that some of the tips and shortcuts that I have described will help you to make easier and better progress than I was able to at times. The work I have done to date has enabled me to be far healthier and more relaxed than I would otherwise have been, and to enjoy quality relationships that years ago I could only have dreamed of. I wish you well on your journey.

Appendix

Resolving problems with alcohol

I have added this subject as an appendix because it is by no means relevant to all readers. It is, however, a very common problem and one that I come across in my therapy room very regularly. Almost without exception, my clients choose not to drink at all after seeing me, and often from the very first session. However, I do not usually address the issue specifically until they have undergone general hypno-analysis for their wider emotional issues. Alcohol is an 'emotional anaesthetic', and I like to start by finding out what the past experiences are that the client wishes to numb.

Why is it so difficult to drink alcohol moderately, or better still, not at all?

In my opinion, there are three types of drinker:

1. The lucky minority who really can take or leave alcohol, and drink well within recommended guidelines.
2. The majority who frequently exceed the guidelines and try with varying degrees of success to moderate their intake. Their consumption usually increases as they get older.

3. The very unlucky minority who drink far more than they should, and whose intake is way out of control.

For many years, I was in the second category. I knew that drinking as much alcohol as I did was not a great idea for health reasons, but it was a behaviour pattern which I, like many people, found really hard to change.

This raises several questions. How can some people remain entirely able to take or leave alcohol, while others find it seemingly addictive? Why are a few people unable to prevent themselves from knowingly drinking themselves into a very early grave? Is there such a thing as an addictive personality? If this describes me, why am I not addicted to anything else? Why did I feel almost compelled to drink at home, but feel no craving at all when I spent ten days climbing Mount Kilimanjaro? None of this made sense to me.

For the record, the current UK alcohol consumption guidelines are now the same for men and women – a maximum of 14 units per week. That equates to roughly one and a half bottles of red wine, or just under two bottles of white. For the first time, the Chief Medical Officer for the UK has stated that there is 'no safe level of alcohol consumption'.

Some years ago, I read Allen Carr's book *The Easy Way to Control Alcohol.*[31] It made some very interesting points, and I would recommend it to anyone who wants to understand this subject in more detail. I refer to some of his ideas here, but in truth, the understanding I gained made no difference to my alcohol consumption. I was forced to assume that, for me at least, there was more to this issue than he described.

Soon after I opened my therapy business, a client asked me to help her to moderate her drinking. As I studied her psychologically, I realised that my emotional background was very similar to hers. I gradually formed an idea of how we had got ourselves into this situation, and from there I planned our escape.

Personally, I think that one of the contributing factors is a subconscious lack of self-love. I think people who lack self-love are much more likely to become alcohol dependent because their innate instinct for self-care is reduced. It is part of our deepest programming to care for those we love, and that should include ourselves. If we lack self-love, we will lack a strong instinct to self-care, and habits which conflict with that instinct are consequently easier to fall into. Before I explain the exact process, let's have a quick look at why drinking alcohol is such a bad idea.

The health effects of drinking alcohol – the downside

Ethyl alcohol is toxic – really toxic - it is totally undrinkable if not significantly diluted with more palatable liquids. The strongest spirits only contain about 40% pure alcohol, and many people find them completely undrinkable. But diluting poison does not make it less poisonous, just less unpalatable - it still seriously damages your body. There is a clue in the word 'intoxicated' – you have taken in a toxin. Let us look at what alcohol actually does.

It unquestionably increases your risk of:

- Cancer - particularly of the mouth, throat, stomach and liver
- Blood clots, strokes and heart attacks
- Liver cirrhosis – this is potentially fatal, and women are especially vulnerable
- Nerve damage leading to muscle weakness, incontinence (and erectile dysfunction in men)
- Memory loss and dementia

It can also cause depression - people claim it's the other way around, but it isn't.

And if this isn't enough, you will also increase the chances of getting gout and high blood pressure, having your immune

239

system suppressed so you are more prone to getting infections, becoming diabetic and/or epileptic, and gaining weight. Oh, and you could well end up with a red blotchy complexion with broken blood vessels, and a swollen nose – not a good look for a man, worse for a woman!

Apart from this, alcoholism contributes to many social problems including violence, breakdown in family relationships, unemployment and homelessness.

The upside of drinking alcohol

In the spirit of fairness, we should consider the other side of the argument. If you think that drinking alcohol relaxes you, this is an illusion. What actually happens is that you get stressed when you crave a drink, and the drink relieves the stress that abstinence caused. It is true that alcohol has a dis-inhibiting effect, but if you look at most people's behaviour when they are thoroughly dis-inhibited, (i.e. drunk!) it's not much of a selling point is it?

You could suggest that getting really drunk relieves stress because it stops your brain from remembering your problems, let alone thinking about them, but there are many better ways of problem-solving and coping with life's challenges than destroying your brain function.

Think about this: if you went to the doctor's and said, 'Doc, I'm struggling with life a bit at the moment – can you give me something to help me cope?' And he said, 'Sure - I've got just the stuff for you – I've got this liquid that you can drink on a daily basis – I have to admit that it is expensive and poisonous, and it will probably kill you in the long run, but in the meanwhile it will just dull your senses, destroy your willpower and generally make you act stupid – oh, and you'll wake up feeling awful whenever you take it – would you like some?' Only an idiot would accept.

Allen Carr suggests an interesting test. Close your eyes and imagine as clearly as you can the taste of your favourite, freshly squeezed fruit juice. Can you honestly say that you prefer the taste of wine or beer to this flavour? I doubt it, but which would you choose at a party? If it's alcohol, ask yourself why.

To understand what has gone wrong here, we need to look in more depth at why you would make what looks like an illogical choice. If you have read this far through the book, you will know that any behaviour which you do not consciously wish to engage in is inevitably driven by your subconscious mind. So the simple answer is that your compulsion to drink alcohol is driven by your subconscious mind - you have inadvertently come to believe, deep down, that you actually *need* to drink alcohol. Let's look at how that could have happened.

How is your body designed to help you not to consume things that are bad for you?

Taste and smell are very closely linked, and although they are both subjective, in general, healthy things taste and smell good, unhealthy things taste and smell bad. So fresh fruit smells good, rotten fruit smells bad. It is still fruit, but your mind has changed your perception from 'nice' to 'nasty' because the fruit has gone from being 'good for you' to being 'bad for you'. So if things smell and taste bad, that is your body's way of telling you to avoid them.

No one I have ever spoken to claimed that alcohol tasted and smelled good when they first started drinking – this is your body trying to dissuade you from consuming it – so to begin with, the system is working. The trouble starts when you choose to repeatedly ignore the message your body is giving you. This is often not just down to peer pressure – it is partly due to our own desire to look 'grown-up' that we persist with the behaviour that our body would like us to stop. We all know that children don't drink alcohol and adults do, so while we are in our teens, we think that drinking alcohol will make others see us as adults. When you analyse it, at this point in your life you deliberately decided to habitually drink a poison that made you act stupid in order to look grown-up – how was that going to work?! I do know of rare cases when children were actually forced to drink alcohol, but this is obviously the exception rather than the rule.

So anyway, you start by drinking shandy, or having spirits with lots of sugary mixers like Coca-Cola, to try and make them palatable, and you pretend to like them. At this point you are ignoring the 'advice' of your subconscious mind which makes you instinctively dislike alcoholic drinks, and you persist in consuming them. Now this is where your body is clever, because if you keep doing something in these circumstances, your body is eventually forced to the conclusion that you can't avoid doing it, so it changes your perception of alcohol from unpalatable to palatable. It does this because there is no biological advantage in making you continue to suffer an unpleasant experience if you genuinely can't avoid the situation.

To understand the biological background to this, imagine that you were on a remote island. There is only one bacteria-infested water supply, and naturally it tastes bad to you because it is clearly unsanitary. But you would have to drink it because you would die if you didn't drink water. Your mind would soon figure this out, and on the assumption that you had no alternative, it would gradually change your perception of the flavour from unpalatable to palatable. At this point, you would have inadvertently taught your subconscious mind that drinking the water was essential to survival and was therefore a desirable behaviour.

By the same process, you learn to tolerate alcohol, and your perception of its flavour consequently changes from unpalatable to palatable. But if you drink too much of it, it still makes you feel dreadful and throw up to eject excesses from the system – your body might have changed your perception of the taste, but alcohol is still a poison which your body cannot tolerate in large quantities. As your body gets better at breaking the alcohol down, by definition, your tolerance of it goes up, so you gradually need to drink more and more to get the same effect. Guess what – you are on a slippery slope! It would be better for us if we continued to puke like teenagers, but your body soon stops doing this because it is trying to help you by adjusting to something which it assumes you must need.

Because of peer pressure, and the fun you tend to have in social situations, you persevere and keep drinking. Your body does its best to adjust because it assumes there is no alternative, but increased tolerance does not mean that your body is coping with being poisoned – it is definitely not. Tolerance increases simply because your body gets better at breaking alcohol down, so you have to drink more to get the same effect, and you always will have to if you keep drinking.

If you increase your consumption still further, your body makes the enzymes necessary to break down alcohol in advance of your drinking. This is why almost everyone who feels any compulsion to drink, gradually increases their consumption as they get older. As your tolerance increases, you often then choose stronger drinks, so you keep putting pressure on your subconscious mind to accept alcohol as unavoidable, *and by implication, necessary.*

This is a crucial point to understand – the compulsion you feel to drink alcohol is a result of you having inadvertently re-programmed your subconscious mind. Because there is no biological advantage in making you dislike something which your subconscious mind now believes you have to consume, your subconscious mind has now changed your perception of alcohol from unpalatable to palatable, and more importantly, you have changed your subconscious belief from thinking that drinking alcohol is undesirable to believing it is **necessary***.*

So to start with, your body was trying to stop you drinking alcohol, and you used your conscious mind to overrule it. At some point, you came to realise that your desire to drink alcohol had become unhealthy, and you wanted to cut back but found it very difficult. Now the tables are turned, and you consciously want to stop, but your subconscious wants you to do it. As we have already learned, the subconscious mind is far more powerful than the conscious mind, and it will always win a battle of wills.

This insight about how alcohol dependency is arrived at is the key to solving the problem – and it can be solved.

As previously mentioned, I believe this process is more likely to happen in people whose instinct to self-care is weakened by a lack of self-love. Furthermore, for the unfortunate few who drink destructively, I would suggest that they may go beyond a lack of self-love, and subconsciously hate themselves – hence the subconscious urge to self-destruct.

Another false connection that our brain makes is to link drinking alcohol with having fun, and this is simply because we usually drink at fun events – eating with friends, socialising, weddings, etc. But it's a false connection – the event would be fun with or without alcohol. It is certainly true that some people relax and laugh more when they are dis-inhibited. In this instance they are using alcohol as a social lubricant, but there are better ways of overcoming shyness. As consumption increases and we see our friends drunk and laughing, they are actually laughing because they are mostly saying and doing stupid things. Alcohol is not known as a substance which improves our decision-making or ability to assess risk! When you think about it, alcohol impairs brain function and temporarily stops you being intelligent. Why would you do that – why not remain intelligent and have a laugh?

Do you think that drinking alcohol is an addiction or a habit?

Let me give you a clue here – biting your nails is a subconsciously-driven habit, but taking heroin is an addiction. Which do you think drinking alcohol is? Allen Carr is very clear on this point and I completely agree with him.

If you think it is an addiction, do you wake up in the night craving more alcohol? Do you have alcohol for breakfast? Would you steal or kill to get the money to buy a drink? If the answer to any of these questions is 'yes', then I would agree that you drink so much that you have an addiction, but for most drinkers the answer is clearly 'no'.

If alcohol were truly addictive, there would be definite withdrawal symptoms if you stopped for a while, not just cravings. There can be withdrawal symptoms for really serious alcoholics, but there aren't for most 'social drinkers'.

This is an appropriate point for a health warning. If you stop drinking alcohol and you feel any adverse effect, mental or physical, you must seek medical attention. Just so that you know what to look out for:

The physical symptoms of withdrawal include hand tremors, sweating, nausea, visual hallucinations, and in extreme cases, seizures.

The mental symptoms include depression, anxiety, irritability, restlessness and insomnia.

I cannot emphasise enough that if you get any of these symptoms as a result of sharply reducing your alcohol consumption, you must drink enough to keep them at bay and seek medical advice.

For the rest of us, the cravings we get to consume alcohol are not a sign of addiction. To understand what they are, think back to Chapter 1 and my comments about habits and triggers. Let me remind you:

One of the functions of the subconscious mind is to recognise routine tasks in our daily lives and automate them wherever possible. It is a great system, unless of course you inadvertently automate a process that you do not wish to continue! If you routinely open and consume a bottle of wine with your evening meal, your mind will soon spot the pattern and it will not be long before you find yourself doing it whether you think it is a good idea or not. The meal becomes the trigger, 'x', and drinking the wine becomes the activity, 'y'.

So my contention is that for most people, drinking alcohol is largely a habit, not an addiction. I first realised this when I spent ten days up Mount Kilimanjaro. There are no pubs or off-licences up there – I certainly didn't spot any. So I was not at home, or in any of my usual drinking environments. Consequently there were no triggers. I can honestly say that I didn't have any craving to drink alcohol at all – it didn't even occur to me that I wasn't drinking.

So if drinking alcohol is a habit, how do you break it?

Well, you have just achieved the first step – seeing it for what it is. If you think you have an addiction, your immediate perception is that stopping will be incredibly difficult. But we all know that habits are less of a challenge. If you change from a manual to an automatic car, for example, you very quickly break the habit of wanting to change gear. You could have changed gear manually a hundred thousand times over the years, but within a day or two, you forget the idea completely. That was a deeply ingrained, fully automated process, and you broke it with ease.

It is actually a complete illusion that habits are hard to break. We need to think they are hard to break in order for them to work, but when we perceive a *need* to be able to break them, we can do it with relative ease.

One of the very interesting points that Allen Carr makes in his book is that the urge to drink alcohol is not like any normal urge. If you are hungry and you eat food, you cease to be hungry – the urge goes away. If you are thirsty, and you drink water, you cease to be thirsty – the urge goes away. If you are horny, and you have sex, you cease to be horny – the urge goes away.

If you want alcohol, and you drink some, the urge doesn't go away, it actually gets stronger, so at that point you either have to torture yourself by being restrained, or you are at the mercy of alcohol again.

Understand that the urge to drink alcohol is not a 'natural urge', and you can never satisfy it.

Do you want to stop drinking, or just moderate your intake?

Frankly, this is a no-brainer for three reasons:

1. If you agree that there is no upside to drinking alcohol, why do it at all? How much sense is there in saying 'I accept that alcohol is poisoning me, so I have decided to drink a little poison rather than a lot'?
2. It is generally agreed that, because alcohol is 'moreish', not drinking at all is easier than drinking moderately. Because of its dis-inhibiting effect, alcohol progressively

destroys your willpower as you consume it, so good intentions at the outset of a drinking session are mostly doomed to fail. Most of us have been in this situation!

3. Moderation is, almost by definition, hard to achieve because alcohol makes you thirstier the more you drink.

Think of being alcohol-free as walking along a straight and level path that is easy to walk along, and off to the side is a slippery slope that starts off on a very slight incline, but gets progressively steeper. And to take the analogy further, imagine that some people have different degrees of grip on the soles of their shoes, so some people slide down the slope quicker than others. You have already demonstrated that your shoes are not very grippy. As evidenced by the fact that most people, probably including you, have a tendency to drink progressively more as they get older, they are all sliding downwards. So in truth, there is only one outcome of being anywhere on that slope – you will slide down - the only variable being how long it will take you to get there.

If you are like most people, you will have already tried hard, on many occasions, to get back up the slippery slope. And sometimes, after a period of struggling, you seem to have slipped down further – am I right? Well, the aim of this chapter is to help you to get back on the level path, where life is easy. Can you see from this analogy that trying to walk along the top of the slope is not a sensible choice? The easiest route is along the path.

So do you stop immediately, or over a period of time?

I will start by re-iterating the safety advice given earlier – if you are a heavy drinker and/or you feel any adverse symptoms at all when you stop drinking for even a short period, you must seek medical advice. As a layman, I do not think that there is a specific level of drinking below which it is safe to just stop, and above which it is not. I assume that this would vary widely between different people – be careful, and sensible.

If you feel that the warning above does not apply to you, and you feel that you could stop immediately, then that is your prerogative. This is what I did, and I felt no adverse effects whatsoever, but my advice remains to seek medical advice if you are in any doubt.

If you want to take a more graduated approach, there are various strategies you could follow which might include:

1. Record accurately your exact alcohol intake on a daily basis. Learn how to calculate units of alcohol if you don't already know. Plot this information on a graph so that you can see a visual representation of your progress at a glance. Draw a straight line on the graph from your

252

current intake to zero over your chosen timescale. Keep the plotted figures under the line and you know you are on target to succeed.

2. Choose a certain number of alcohol-free days per week, and stick to them. Make it the same days every week – you are making a new habit. Avoid known triggers on those days. Give yourself alternative treats to look forward to. Gradually increase the number of alcohol-free days.

3. Choose less alcoholic drinks – white wine instead of red, spritzers, weaker lager, more mixers, etc.

4. Drink a significant amount of water before you drink alcohol so that you are made to feel less thirsty.

5. Start drinking later in the day, or go to bed earlier.

6. Don't keep alcohol in the house – if you haven't got it, you can't be tempted to drink it!

7. Think before you drink – do you **really** want alcohol, or would you rather have your health, a clear head and self-respect?

8. On alcohol-free days, before you even get up in the morning, visualise being healthy, energetic and proud of being alcohol-free. Make it as real as possible. Visualise people congratulating you on your strength of mind. Visualise going to bed sober and proud of it – picture all of the benefits: increased self-respect, better health, a

sharper mind, pride in yourself. Visualisation is an extremely powerful tool. You can use this tool just as much if you stop instantly, rather than over a period.

Stopping gradually doesn't necessarily mean stopping slowly – it just means not instantly - you could still achieve it in a week or two. As long as the trend is downwards, you are succeeding, and that in itself empowers you further. You will not be breaking a habit, so much as gradually changing it for a different habit.

As I mentioned earlier, I stopped instantly and in all honestly I didn't really even have any cravings. How did I achieve this? Firstly, understanding the psychological process that got me into this situation made a huge difference. This is why I have explained it in detail, and it is effectively what Cognitive Behavioural Therapy is about. Looking in depth at the problem, and breaking it down into manageable pieces, understanding that I was not an addict, knowing that cravings are really just an illusion created by the subconscious mind, understanding that habits are definitely breakable, avoiding triggers where possible, having substitute 'treats', telling my friends what I was doing so that I was less likely to backslide, using creative visualisation. Last but not least, learning to love myself – as previously described.

The good news is that you don't have to stop for long and your tolerance and perception return to normal, because, as you now know, your body is capable of constant self-adjustment and change. Habits get weaker and weaker until you are completely unaware of them.

I did not use hypnosis to help myself, but I do with clients. This is because I spent so long studying the situation that my thoughts on the subject became deeply ingrained, but with clients, I have to achieve the same outcome in an hour or two. As you now know, hypnosis gives us the opportunity to turn conscious thoughts into deeply held 'core beliefs'. Most clients report that when their subconscious urge is congruent with their conscious desires, they experience little or no cravings to drink alcohol at all.

Other people's reactions

Allen Carr quite correctly points out that when you stop, other people's reactions will be split.

The people who really care about you will be delighted, and you will unquestionably earn their respect – so there's another pay-off. It is without doubt an excellent decision for your family, and they will see the benefits, both short- and long-term: better health, better behaviour, more money, longer lifespan. Why wouldn't they be delighted about that?

But there will be drinking buddies who may not like it, and that is simply because your success has underlined their own shortcomings – your ability to stop has highlighted their own inability to do the same thing. Secretly, they will respect you too, but they will never admit it. They may well try and test your resolve, but if you give in, you will lose your self-respect and theirs. Don't be superior, don't try and convert them, just know you have made the right choice, and keep your resolve. Avoid their company for a while if you need to.

What next? A word of warning

At this point you have every right to be proud of yourself – you have achieved something which millions of people try to do and fail. It really is an achievement, but do not fall into the trap of thinking that you have gained control and mastery over alcohol, and that you can now take it or leave it at will. What you have done, using your intellect and willpower, is to get off the slippery slope and onto the level path at the top. Do not think that this qualifies you to get back on the slippery slope and somehow enables you to stay near the top – you will still slide down just like everybody else.

This is a common trap – do not fall into it!

Converting volumes and percentages to units of alcohol.

In the UK, one 'unit' equates to 10mls of pure ethyl alcohol. To calculate consumption, multiply the volume of the bottle or can in litres (i.e. 0.75 for a 75cl bottle of wine, or 0.33 for a 330ml bottle of beer) by the percentage of alcohol.

I.e. a 750cc bottle of 13% proof red wine will be 0.75 x 13 = 9.75 units. A bottle of red is therefore about 10 units, and a bottle of 11% proof white is about 8 units. A 440ml can of 4.5% proof lager is therefore 2 units

Case study – Sean

Most of the case studies in this book have been a short overview of cases which demonstrate particular examples of points I am making in the text. This case study explains the therapy of an alcoholic in his own words:

After drinking every week for 30 years, I started to notice that it had become a daily routine. I increasingly found that I needed to drink to relax – on a typical evening I might drink six gin and tonics and a bottle of wine, and double that on weekends. Despite having lost several close friends to alcoholism, I found it impossible to reduce my intake to a healthier level using willpower. I decided I needed help.

I chose hypnotherapy, and was surprised to find that it was both enjoyable and fascinating. I learned that every adult carries with them some kind of

'baggage' from their past — what most people don't realise is the ongoing influence that this baggage can have on their day-to-day behaviour. It made perfect sense when Richard explained to me that anything I did which I did not consciously want to do, like drinking alcohol excessively, was driven by my subconscious mind.

After just one session I felt so much better, and after the third session I was finished, and ready to take on the world. Richard's advice, based on medical grounds, was to reduce my alcohol intake over several months, but I decided to just stop. I have not had an alcoholic drink since, and I have no desire to have one. Having resolved the subconscious desire to drink, it does not even take willpower to stay 'dry'. I still take clients out to lunch, and go to the pub with friends, but I drink lime and soda. I feel totally relaxed doing so, and wake up hangover-free and with money in my pocket.

I don't miss drinking alcohol, and I enjoy being a better version of myself. The biggest differences I have found are that my relationships with my wife and my daughter have improved, I sleep better, I have more energy and self-respect, and I have lost weight — so the money I have saved by not drinking will need to be spent on new clothes!

Thank you Richard for all your help — you are a real gentleman.

Can you achieve this without professional help?

The answer is obviously yes, because plenty of people have, but it will be much easier if, with the help of a hypno-analyst, you first resolve the emotional issues which got you into this situation in the first place.

Bibliography

1 Sigmund Freud, *The Psychopathology of Everyday Life*, new ed. (London: Penguin Modern Classics, 2002).

2 Norman Doidge, *The Brain that Changes Itself*, UK ed. (London: Penguin Books, 2008).

3 David Eagleman, *Incognito: The Secret Lives of the Brain*, UK ed. (Edinburgh: Canongate Books, 2012).

4 Lucia Capacchione, *Recovery of Your Inner Child: The Highly Acclaimed Method for Liberating Your Inner Self* (New York: Simon & Schuster, 1991).

5 Sigmund Freud, *Group Psychology and the Analysis of the Ego*, 3rd ed. (London: Hogarth Press, 1945).

6 Gabor Maté, *When the Body Says No: Exploring the Stress-Disease Connection* (New Jersey: John Wiley & Sons, 2013).

7 Bruce H. Lipton, *The Biology of Belief: Unleashing The Power Of Consciousness, Matter & Miracles*, UK ed.(London: Hay House, 2011).

8 Eric Berne, *Transactional Analysis in Psychotherapy: A Systematic Individual and Social Psychiatry*, reprint ed. (Eastford, CT: Martino Fine Books, 2015).

9 David Indermaur, 'Young Australians and Domestic Violence', *Trends and Issues in Crime and Criminal Justice*, no. 195 (Canberra: 2001); Miriam K. Ehrensaft et al, 'Clinically Abusive Relationships in an Unselected Birth Cohort: Men's and Women's Participation and Developmental Antecedents', *Journal of Abnormal Psychology*, vol. 113, no. 2 (Washington DC: 2004); WHO, 'World Report on Violence and Health', ed. by Etienne G. Krug et al (Geneva: 2002); Nilar Kyu and Atsuko Kanai, 'Prevalence, Antecedent Causes and Consequences of Domestic Violence in Myanmar', *Asian Journal of Social Psychology*, vol. 8 (Singapore: 2005).

10 *Desert Island Discs*, 2012 [radio]. BBC Radio 4. 28 October. 11:15.

11 Dale Carnegie, *How to Win Friends and Influence People*, new ed. (London: Vermilion, Ebury, 2006).

12 Olivia Fox Cabane, *The Charisma Myth: Master the Art of Personal Magnetism*, UK ed. (London: Portfolio Penguin, 2013).

13 Sigmund Freud, *Three Essays on the Theory of Sexuality*, reprint ed. (Eastford, CT: Martino Fine Books, 2011).

14 Terence Watts, *Warriors, Settlers and Nomads: Discovering Who We Are and What We Can Be* (Carmarthen: Crown House Publishing, 2000).

15 Laurens Van Der Post, *The Lost World of the Kalahari*, new ed. (London: Vintage Classics, 2002).

16 Judith Orloff, *Emotional Freedom*, reprint ed. (New York: Three Rivers Press, 2010).

17 Oliver James, *Not in Your Genes: The Real Reasons Children Are Like Their Parents* (London: Vermilion, Ebury, 2016)

[18] Christiane Beerlandt, *The Key to Self-liberation: 1000 Diseases and Their Psychological Origins*, UK ed. (Altina, 2003)

[19] Debbie Shapiro, *Your Body Speaks Your Mind: Understanding How Your Emotions and Thoughts Affect You Physically* (London: Piatkus, 1996)

[20] Louise Hay, *Heal Your Body: The Mental Causes for Physical Illness*, 4th ed. (London: Hay House, 2004

[21] A. J. de Craen, P. J. Roos, A. Leonard de Vries et al, 'Effect of colour of drugs: systematic review of perceived effect of drugs and of their effectiveness', *The BMJ*, vol. 313 (London: 1996)

[22] Gary Holz, *Secrets of Aboriginal Healing: A Physicist's Journey with a Remote Australian Tribe*, 2nd ed. (Rochester, VA: Bear & Company, 2013).

[23] David R. Hamilton, *It's The Thought That Counts: Why Mind Over Matter Really Works*, revised ed. (London: Hay House, 2008).

[24] Patricia Worby, *The Scar that Won't Heal: Stress, Trauma and Unresolved Emotion in Chronic Disease* (CreateSpace, 2015).

[25] Shakti Gawain, *Creative Visualization*, new ed. (San Fransisco, CA: New World Library, 2002).

[26] Hyman Judah Schachtel, *The Enjoyment of Living* (New York: Dutton, 1954).

[27] Dave Elman, *Hypnotherapy* (Glendale, CA: Westwood Publishing Co, 1984).

[28] Candace Pert, *The Molecules of Emotion: Why You Feel the Way You Feel*, new ed. (London: Simon & Schuster, 1999).

[29] P. K. House, A. Vyas, R. Sapolsky, 'Predator Cat Odors Activate Sexual Arousal Pathways in Brains of Toxoplasma gondii Infected Rats', *PLOS One*, 6 (8) (San Fransisco, CA: 2011).

[30] Yuval Noah Harari, *Sapiens: A Brief History of Humankind* (London: Harvill Secker, 2014).

[31] Allen Carr, *The Easy Way to Control Alcohol*, 2nd ed. (London: Arcturus Publishing, 2009).

42947399R00150

Printed in Poland
by Amazon Fulfillment
Poland Sp. z o.o., Wrocław